DOMESTIC
AFFAIRS

DOMESTIC AFFAIRS

Miriam Finkelstein

Boston

Houghton Mifflin Company

1982

Library of Congress Cataloging in Publication Data

Finkelstein, Miriam.
Domestic affairs.

I. Title.
PS3556.I483D6   813'.54   81-6887
ISBN 0-395-31822-X   AACR2

Printed in the United States of America

S   10   9   8   7   6   5   4   3   2   1

For Jim and Anne and David

DOMESTIC
AFFAIRS

THEY HAD HAD A LONG DISCUSSION the night before about whether or not she should come with him to the airport. "Don't bother," Tom had said irritably, watching Laura as she slid pieces of tissue paper between his shirts and placed the neat balls of his socks in the corners of the suitcase. "There's no need to come."

"But I want to come," she said. It was almost as if she would not really believe that he was leaving unless she saw his plane take off.

He asked if she wanted to accompany him on the subway, knowing she would not. He had planned to take the special subway line that went directly to Kennedy. She asked him please to take a taxi. It would be much more convenient, especially with the luggage. He agreed as a concession to her. But he wanted it clear that he was being magnanimous, that he really much preferred the other route.

Since the children had left for camp and the single ticket to Geneva had arrived in the mail, they had been like this with each other. Warily polite, like major powers at the bargaining table. Or rather at the banquet table. After she finished the packing they had gone together to their favorite

Szechuan restaurant, shared hot and sour soup, special tidbits from the steaming metal-domed dishes ("Have you tried this? It's very good. I think you'd like it"), both watching carefully for double meanings, for signs of remorse or of pique. They had not been so aware of each other in a long time.

At night, they slept on the outer edges of their double bed, defying the forces of marital gravity that pushed them toward the hollow in the center. If their hips had touched in the middle of the night they would have murmured, like Alphonse and Gaston, "Oh pardon me." "No, no, pardon me. My fault entirely."

In the morning it was a relief to have so many things to do. Outside, the city was already baking in an early summer heat wave. The humidity had turned her usual short brown curls into a frizzy mass, but there was no time to untangle it now. The cab would be downstairs at ten o'clock. They had allowed an hour's extra time for catastrophes on the Van Wyck Expressway.

She put on her lightest and loosest clothes, an Indian print skirt and a sheer cotton blouse that Tom had once said he liked. He stepped out of the shower and stared at her, as if he couldn't remember who she was, or what she was doing in his bedroom. She looks nice in that outfit, he thought. Younger and sexier — like someone it would be fun to go on a trip with.

It was getting late. He burrowed into his bureau drawer, looking for his shorts, then found them on top where Laura had left them for him.

Covertly, as she packed his toothbrush and electric razor in his flight bag, she looked at his long lean body. Even though the hair on the top of his head was getting thin (she could see the bald spot as he rummaged in the bureau drawer), everywhere else on his body it grew thick and luxuriantly. The first time she had seen him naked she had been surprised. Clothed, he had somehow not had the aura of such a richly hairy man.

There really wasn't time for such thoughts. Tom was buttoning up his shirt, tying his tie, looking at his watch. In the cab on the way to the airport, he reminded her that he would call from Switzerland every Friday night to see how she was doing.

"I might be out."

"Where would you be?" he said. "I'll call at ten. You'll be back by then."

She pointed out that it would be three o'clock in the morning in Geneva. He said he would call anyway, since it seemed to be the most convenient time for her.

Hot winds filled with particles of sand swept across their faces, as they got out of the cab. Fortunately the terminal was cool. Also full of people in a hurry, scurrying down the long concrete corridors, canvas satchels slung over their shoulders, ticket folders clutched in their hands. Suddenly Laura felt excluded. Tom was about to walk through the door marked, "FOR DEPARTING PASSENGERS ONLY," and she was not. The fact that it was her decision, not his, was irrelevant. It would be better to leave before that moment came. "Tom, I think we'd better say good-bye now."

He looked surprised, then leaned down to kiss her. They clutched each other with an intensity they had not known for several months. His mustache tickled her upper lip, as it always did. Their second kiss was remote, as if they were already apart.

As she boarded the creaky airport bus heading back toward the steaming city, she realized it was the first time in twelve years that she had been in New York without Tom or the children. The month of July stretched in front of her, invitingly empty of obligations. She felt as if she were the one about to embark on an overseas adventure.

Laura had no detailed plan, no secret list of activities she had been prevented from doing by the presence of her husband and children. No matter what Tom thought. The real reason she was not going to Geneva with him was much simpler. She wanted to find out if she could propel herself from one day to the next without the constant push of other people's needs.

When she had first come to New York as a newly married woman, she had wanted Tom always close by her side. She was attached to him by the powerful bonds of recently discovered sexual passion. Besides, he had grown up in the city and knew its odd ways. Now she wanted to see what it would be like to explore the city by herself.

Just behind her eyes she felt the possibility of the emergence of a new personality. Or the re-emerging of several old ones. In any case, she was tired of the person she knew so well, the competent organized woman who made lists. She had been organized for a long time now, ever since her marriage. Everything in its proper place, or at least on its proper list.

In the apartment, her domain, she was the queen of all objects. "Mom, somebody stole my raincoat." Or, "Laura, where are my car keys?" Like a sorcerer she would tell Tom his keys were on top of the TV set, then flick the missing raincoat from the pile at the bottom of the closet. There were occasional flaws in her omniscience. For instance, she could never find her own pocketbook. The others were happy to find it for her, the three of them prowling through the house like big-game hunters, while she stood helpless in the front hall, unable to go out.

She also left her family notes on the bulletin board about chores to be done. She expected them to let her know where they were at all times, and if they would be late for dinner. Mostly they did, but sometimes Tom would decide that, as chief breadwinner, the rules didn't apply to him, and he would come home late without letting her know. She would worry, even scream a bit when he finally appeared. "It was unavoidable," he would say, as if this were an explanation, and retreat behind his newspaper like a knight behind a shield.

Enough thinking about Tom. She had nobody's time to organize now but her own, and not even that if she didn't want to. She looked at the other passengers on the bus. People in New York looked more interesting in the summer. Emerging from the heavy coats and boots of winter, the raincoats and ponchos of the long rainy spring, they burst forth like butterflies, their bodies clothed in Day-Glo tops, see-through blouses, tight jeans, and shorts. Even toes were visible, no longer encased in boots and clogs.

The couple on her right were talking excitedly in a language she didn't recognize. Not Spanish and not Yiddish. Maybe it was Russian. Something Slavic anyway — much like the fake guttural language that she and her best friend, Rachel, used to scream at each other on hot summer afternoons.

The bus was now hurtling down the highway at an alarming rate. The driver seemed to think that he was driving a taxi. She turned her attention to the young couple sitting on her left. The woman was wearing cutoff jeans and a halter made from a red silk scarf, her nipples visible through the silk. The man's purple T-shirt said MOSTLY MOZART. They were talking about what they would eat for supper. New Yorkers were always talking about food. Restaurants, recipes, places to buy ethnic specialties. When she came to New York it was one of the first differences she had noticed.

The woman was saying sulkily, "You can buy them if you want to. But I won't eat them."

The man replied teasingly, but insistently. "But I want you to eat them."

She tossed her long black hair out of her eyes and stared out the window of the bus as if the apartment houses of Queens were of immense interest to her. Finally she said, "It's not that I have any objections to eating them. I just don't understand why you care so much."

He leaned forward and nibbled her. "I told you. Because they'll make you sexier."

Laura leaned forward, pretending to tighten the strap of her sandal, trying to hear, but they were now whispering in each other's ears and giggling. What food were they talking about? She was consumed with curiosity.

Maybe she should get some. After all, she could eat whatever she wanted, whenever she wanted to. She no longer had to check with Tom and Kathy and Jeff to make sure that the menu was acceptable to each of them, and also to the white-coated nutritionist who lived in her head. The refrigerator at home was almost bare.

As was the bulletin board next to the telephone in the kitchen. On it were only the phone number of the camp where the children were immured, and Jeffrey's carefully typed instructions on the care and feeding of Harold, his hamster. No lists of chores, errands, or appointments.

It was unsettling, but also exciting. After all, she hadn't been abandoned. The children had gone to camp for the last two summers. And Tom had wanted her to go with him to the industrial chemists' conference in Geneva. In fact he had made it quite clear that he expected her to go.

"You can go by yourself," she had told him. "I'm planning to stay in New York this time."

At first he had not believed her. "But of course you're coming, Laura. You went last year. And the year before."

"This year I'm not." She was surprised at how fast her heart was beating. Had it been so long since she had said no to something he wanted her to do? "It's my turn. I need some time to myself."

When he saw she was serious, he made the one plea that he seemed to feel would surely reach her. "I'll be very lonely without you."

Would he? Would she? That was one of the things she wanted to find out. They had spent so little time apart that they couldn't be sure how they might feel on their own. Funny, she even thought about separation in the plural.

The discussion (a polite word for it — it was the closest they had come to a quarrel in years) simmered on the back burner of their domestic life for the next few weeks. It boiled over at unexpected times.

In the car on their way to a dinner party with old friends, Tom suddenly said, "All the other men will have their wives in Geneva." He sounded so much like their ten-year-old son when he was trying to persuade them to let him go somewhere that Laura burst out laughing. She pointed out that during conferences in Geneva they were rarely together. He was either at meetings or official banquets. She edited manuscripts alone in their hotel room, or accompanied the other men's wives on guided tours to parts of the city she had already seen.

At the dinner table their hostess separated them instantly, assuming they would have nothing to say to each other, and the discussion about Geneva was dropped. Only to burst forth a few nights later in bed, after their usual twice-a-week lovemaking. Tom sat on the side of the bed, pulling on his pajama bottoms. "What is there you want to do in New York that you couldn't do with me here?"

Laura was suddenly very angry. "I might have known you would think that." She moved to her side of the bed (for some reason they always made love on his side) and turned her back. They both pretended to be asleep until they were.

Somehow she had not foreseen the pain her decision would cause him. Several times she noticed him looking at her in a hurt, speculative way. In the midst of a discussion about whether to hire a baby sitter for Saturday, he said accusingly, "Maybe you'd rather not go out with me at all." One evening, when she was hanging the laundry on the ancient wooden rack that constantly threatened to fold up on itself, he had embraced her from behind, putting his arms around her waist and pressing his body against her. She had turned around in surprise, her hands still full of wet socks, but he was already gone.

That night she was tempted to change her mind, to give in, but she did not. An idea planted so casually by an insurance agent's remark a few months ago had now taken root, giving her a stubbornness that startled both of them.

"If the unexpected should happen," the agent had said to Tom in their living room, "where would Mrs. Stone go?"

In the kitchen Laura paused, soapy goblet in hand. Tom's reply was immediate. "She'd go to California to be near her sister."

Tom dead. They were discussing it coolly, practically, as if they were talking about a car loan, or next year's vacation plans. She felt a chill even though steam was rising from the hot water in the sink.

A chill followed by a stab of indignation. How did Tom know where she might or might not go? They had never discussed the question. What made him so sure she would go anywhere? She liked New York; it had been a long struggle out of the suburbs of her childhood and into the city, and she was damned if she was going to be so swiftly moved out of it by two men smugly planning her future in her own living room. What made her maddest was their assumption that she would have to go somewhere, that she couldn't possibly stay where she was if Tom weren't there too. That she had to be under some relative's supervision.

That night she had watched Tom as he slept, monitoring each rise and fall of his chest as if she were the night nurse in the intensive care unit. Once, as he turned, his breath stopped for a second, and hers stopped too.

Tonight she would be sleeping in their bed alone. Tom would be in a bed in a hotel room in Geneva. She had a sudden picture of Kathy and Jeff asleep in their junior girl and intermediate boy bunks in Camp Tumbleweed. Tonight no two members of the family would be sleeping under the same roof. A non-nuclear family.

She would not really be alone. She knew people in the city — women to have dinner with, to go to matinees and museums with. And she had manuscripts to edit.

The bus was moving more slowly now as it approached Manhattan. The skyscrapers of midtown were visible for a minute, behind a shimmering blanket of smog and sunlight, before the bus plunged into the Queens Midtown Tunnel. She felt as if she were about to enter the city for the first time.

∞ 2 ∞

THE FIRST WEEK SHE SLEPT LATE, cleaned the closets, bought a new strapless sundress, returned it and bought another one with straps, had lunches and dinners with friends. She saw two foreign movies she had wanted to see that Tom didn't (one was in French; the other, in Polish, made her cry).

On the evening before the Fourth she and Lydia went to Joan of Arc Park where they watched fireworks erupting over the Hudson River. Rockets, Catherine wheels, and Roman candles whooshing up in spirals of dazzling color. The final burst of sound had been so deafening that she put her fingers in her ears. Firecrackers exploded all around them. It was as if they were in the midst of an enemy barrage. "If only I could paint like that," Lydia said enviously.

On Friday Laura went to Wickerson and Lowe to pick up her manuscripts. It was a small publishing house with a long history. She had worked there first as a reader, then as an editor, until Jeff was born. Today the usual Victorian calm of the office was shattered. A manuscript was missing, one that was needed immediately. Secretaries, mailboys, even editors, dashed frantically back and forth, riffled through piles of papers, opened desk drawers at random.

II

For several minutes Laura was unable to get anyone's attention. She was beginning to wonder whether it would be better to go downstairs and telephone, when an editor she knew hurried by. "Mr. Wickerson's out," he said, looking through his pockets as if the manuscript might be lurking in his clothes. (Mr. Wickerson was usually out. Laura had not actually seen him for many years.) "I'll tell Mr. Lowe you're here."

Mr. Lowe seemed unruffled by the confusion. He beamed as he handed her the manuscripts. "We saved these two for you," he said. "They need your special touch. By the beginning of August." She knew his next lines almost by heart. "When are we going to persuade you to come back and work full time?"

Her answer was as rehearsed as his question. "Not yet. Maybe when the children are older."

On her way home, she found herself almost automatically in Zabar's, surrounded by housewives purchasing delicacies for their families. Automatically, she took a number and stood in front of the meat counter. Inside the glass cases were sausages and salamis from all parts of the world. Over her head dangled collanders, kettles, couscous steamers, a ceramic cow — really a milk pitcher — hanging by one foot. On either side of her, eager delicatessen lovers pressed forward, waiting for their numbers to come up.

"Sixty-eight."

She had seventy-one. She thrust the small slip of paper into the hand of a startled man. "Here, take this. I won't be needing it."

Safe once more on the sidewalk, she wondered whether she should have bought some walnut Gourmandaise, a cheese that no one else in the family liked, or perhaps a flaky croissant. No. She knew she was right to have left. Zabar's was part of her winter wife-and-mother-of-two life. She wanted this summer to be different.

That night, Tom's first Friday phone call was brief. He said he was fine. She said she was too. He asked if she was bored. No, of course she wasn't bored. It had, after all, been only a week. She wondered, was it hot in Geneva? Tom sounded annoyed. "Of course not. It's never hot in Geneva."

Mercifully, the operator interrupted saying there was another call for Mr. Stone, and they had had to hang up. Lying in bed, listening to the beat of the Upper West Side bongo drums, she began to wonder who had been calling him so urgently in the middle of the night. But he was in Geneva, three thousand miles away, and there was no way she could find out what he was really doing, so she fell asleep. (Only later did it occur to her that this line of reasoning also applied to her.)

The second week she stopped making grocery lists before she went to the supermarket. In fact she stopped going to the supermarket. It seemed silly to stand in a long line with her container of cottage cheese and a box of blueberries. She stopped calling her friends to make dates for lunch and dinner. She had seen most of them the week before, and what was there to say? She began wandering into movies in the middle of pictures, without having checked the time. In the past she had not been able to bear the suspense of not knowing whether the missing clue was deliberately left out for everybody, or had already been given in the first half of the picture. She discovered now that it gave an added dimension of ambiguity to the plot that she liked.

The first clear-cut indicator that her personality might be changing came in the Korean fruit and vegetable store. Since the others had gone, and especially since her visit to Zabar's, she and the hamster had become almost entirely vegetarian. She realized that she had grown to resent the slabs of beef and lamb skulking in the refrigerator. Now when she opened the door she saw pale green lettuce, rosy tomatoes, beige mushrooms, deep purple eggplant, bright yellow squash.

One hot afternoon as she picked up the last shopping basket

from the sidewalk outside the store, she saw that it already contained six apples in a plastic bag. She hesitated, then tipped the fruit into the box with the other apples (a few rolled in among the melons), took the now-empty basket, and began to shop. She was standing in the line a few minutes later when a thin red-faced woman stormed angrily up to the cash register.

"Where's my package?"

Uncomprehending stares.

"The one I left up front."

Still no response. Now she was exasperated. "I left a bag of apples in the basket right out front. Now it's gone."

Laura said nothing, watching the woman's increasing fury as the owner and his son scurried outside to hunt for the missing apples. She watched as the woman finally gave up, picked up a new basket and began once more to paw at the fruit. In the past she would have felt nervous, guilty. Now to her surprise, she felt gleeful. She and the other people on the line exchanged the shorthand glance that meant "crazy lady" among New Yorkers.

At home, as she lovingly shaped cantaloupe balls for her supper, she began to wonder if she were reverting to an earlier personality. She remembered that at college she had been considered quixotic, impractical — the one who couldn't boil water, or figure out how to work the washer and drier in the basement.

Her college friends had considered her incompetence a lovable trait. They would have been disappointed if she had suddenly become able to manage the details of day-to-day living by herself. She remembered a few years ago, when her ex-roommate Charlotte had appeared in New York on her way to her new husband in Afghanistan. At lunch Laura had clawed futilely at the sugar container, trying to get the sugar to come out, and Charlotte had smiled at her fondly. "Here, let me." Deftly she slid back the little metal tab so that sugar descended in a smooth, even shower. Laura had felt angry, humiliated. Why had she not noticed the little metal trap door? Charlotte had only beamed, her memories of Laura reconfirmed.

It had been a long time since she had had trouble with ordinary procedures. Only a few she still found difficult. Like taking subways, or buckling seatbets. Whenever she pulled, the belt lunged forward a few inches, then refused to move further, or jumped back into its hole like a frightened ferret, only to be dislodged easily by Tom, who said, "It's simple. Here, watch me, and next time you'll be able to do it by yourself."

But these were exceptions in the list of the many things she could now do and do well (in addition to editing manuscripts and writing copy, which she had always been able to do) such as shop, cook, organize shelves and closets, arrange appointments on the telephone, make interesting dinner table conversation with people that she didn't like.

On Tuesday morning of her third week alone Lydia called. "Please don't forget the opening. It's on Saturday."

The announcement was on her desk, where she had carefully placed it when it arrived, thinking that she would probably be in Geneva. "Of course I'm coming." She loved Lydia's huge bright paintings, which for ten years she had shown almost furtively to her friends. ("I just finished this. It's nothing much. What do you think?") And now she was willing to display them in public for non-friends, for strangers and art critics to see. It was an important occasion, and Laura planned to be there.

"Where is the gallery?" she asked.

"In Soho. It's on Prince Street."

Prince Street. There was only one sensible way to get there. The subway that she had avoided for almost a year. The subway, with its noise and graffiti, and the fact, most terrifying of all, that it sometimes stopped between stations, and there was no way to get out, no way at all, until it mysteriously started moving again.

She wasn't exactly sure when she had stopped being able to ride the subways. When she first came to New York she had taken them everywhere. But sometime around the time the children had started school and she was left alone in the apartment, waiting for their return, she had begun to dislike underground travel. She began to ride the subway less and less, until finally she had stopped altogether.

If Tom were here, he could drive her. The show would still be on when he came back. But she wanted to be there on the first day, the opening, when good friends gathered to give their love and support.

Maybe she could get a taxi. No, that was cowardice. Besides, it would cost a fortune. The bus? She had often taken the Riverside Drive bus to lectures at the New School or restaurants in the Village, telling herself that she did it because she liked its long meandering route, the time to think and to speculate on the relationships between the other passengers. (People on the subway had no relationships. They shut themselves up in their heads, alert only to the unexpected move, the sudden thrust of a hand in or out of a pocket.)

In order not to think about the problem, she fished out one of the manuscripts Mr. Lowe had given her and began to read. It was a vampire novel with a special twist. The vampire was a homosexual who attacked only men. Where had Mr. Lowe gotten the idea it was her sort of book? She edited the first fifty pages, restraining herself from taking out all the gory parts. Then she wrote long letters to her children, full of admonitions, rewrote them, adding charming anecdotes and taking out most of the admonitions. She kept herself busy, not wanting to leave too much time to wonder about what she would do.

On Friday afternoon she began cleaning out the spice cabinet, something she hadn't done for several years. In the back of the cabinet she found a giant bottle of garlic powder she had bought on sale a long time ago. Only a little had been used. If a recipe called for garlic she usually chopped or mashed a fresh clove. At this rate, they would all be dead before the bottle was used up.

It was absurd to be outlived by one's spices. On an impulse she picked up the bottle and threw it into the garbage. She took all the ancient oregano, rosemary, and basil and dumped them in too. Tomorrow she would buy small bottles of strong new spices. Or better yet, she would buy seeds and a window box and grow her own herbs, as she had always meant to do.

Then she remembered. Tomorrow. The reception was from two to four-thirty. That night when Tom called she told him about it. His voice over the long distance wires was carefully neutral. "How are you going to get there?"

"I haven't decided yet. Could you give me the number, the one that tells you how to get places by subway?" She knew he would know it, even in Switzerland, and she wrote the number down. Just before he hung up he said, "Somehow I have the feeling you're not going to make it."

Saturday was hazy and hot, the air quality obviously un-acceptable even aboveground. She retreated to the bedroom and the air-conditioner. All Saturday morning the number was busy, only a recording telling her to be patient. At last at one-thirty, a human voice. "Prince Street? I'll have to look that one up." A long wait, then, "Take the IRT to Times Square, change for the BMT-RR, and get off at Prince Street. Then walk west."

BMT-RR? It was hard for her to believe that a train with such unlikely initials could take her any place she really wanted to go. Outside her window she could see people on the streets, walking very slowly as if in a heat trance, steaming sleepwalkers waiting to be awakened by the first cool breeze of September. She dressed slowly. She spent almost twenty minutes looking for her pocketbook. By the time she joined the sun-drugged procession up the block, past the bodega, the Chinese laundry, the plant store, it was two-thirty. Lydia must already be wondering why she wasn't there. A cab or a bus would cause her to miss the opening almost entirely.

As she made her way down the subway stairs a crowd of people surged upward. All these people had ridden on the subway and emerged unscathed, and she could too. She pushed her token into the slot and plunged on, like Alice down the rabbit hole.

For a long time, while she stood a careful distance away from the edge of the platform as if a step forward would send her over the edge, no trains came. Then the sudden thunder of the express. The doors opened and she got on. The walls, floors, even some of the seats were covered with purple, black, and orange scrawls. In the corner two men with glazed eyes watched each other suspiciously. A group of teen-age boys came through from the next car, laughing and pushing each other, looking around as if sizing up the passengers. The doors to the car were still open and she walked out, her legs trembling.

The local had just pulled up across the platform, and she made herself keep going. As she took a seat in the middle of the car, the doors closed behind her and the train screeched out of the station. These people looked more ordinary, less threatening. She should have remembered that taking the local helped. If she found she couldn't stay, there was always the next stop, only a few minutes away.

She took out her book and began to read. The next time she looked up the sign said TIMES SQUARE. She leaped out and began the long trek through the tunnels to the BMT. She was beginning to enjoy her adventure. It was almost like a tale out of the Brothers Grimm — the quest, the obstacles along the way. She made her way through the confusing forest of signs, peering ahead for the magic initials and special arrows that would take her to the next stop on her underground journey. Glimpses of token-sellers behind barred grates, enticing signs saying FROZEN CUSTARD, CHEAP UMBRELLAS,

EXIT TO THE STREET. She ignored them all and kept on walking. At last the platform with others already waiting, people going downtown as she was, or perhaps even to Brooklyn.

Suddenly it seemed a very commonplace thing to be doing. A group of teen-age girls stared at her. One pointed at her skirt and smiled. She realized that they were admiring it, a paisley print that came almost to her ankles, bought in that first week of frantic shopping. She nodded and smiled back at them.

Through the turnstile, up the stairs, and out into the boiling sunshine of Prince and Broadway. Then west, still following the voice on the telephone until it led her safely to her goal.

The gallery was filled with people drinking wine and cold cider. The paintings that she had admired on Lydia's living room walls blazed forth, twice as beautiful on the huge whitewashed walls of the gallery. There was Lydia herself, sweating in an African caftan, looking nervous and happy. "Laura, I'm so glad you came."

Lydia's sister thrust a pen at her. "Sign here. It's not the gallery book, just a personal list of the people who are here." She wrote her name carefully, then walked around the gallery slowly, enjoying each picture. Maybe she would buy one of the smaller ones, put it on the wall over her desk.

"Laura, how did you get here?" asked Caroline, a friend of Lydia's, her T-shirt flaunting her not-so-young breasts. "Did you come by car?"

"No, I came by subway."

Caroline looked remorseful. "I should have called you. You live only a few blocks from me. I could have taken you in my car. It's air-conditioned."

Laura laughed. "Well, you can give me a ride back." No reason to overdo it.

In the car Caroline asked Laura where Tom was, informed her that Michael and Barbara had just separated for the third time but this time it looked permanent, and suggested that perhaps they could go to a movie together.

The sense of pleasure in her subway accomplishment stayed with her for a few days. On Broadway as she walked along swinging her straw bag she thought, "If I could do that and even enjoy it, who knows what I might not do?"

A young man waved a bunch of fliers about a cleaning service in her face. "Madam, do you have carpets?"

Without breaking stride she said triumphantly over her shoulder, "No!" (A lie — she did have one in the living room.)

He called after her. "Furniture?"

By that time she was too far away for him to hear, so she answered in her head, "No, nothing. I eat and sleep on the floor."

∞ *3* ∞

SHE BECAME A SUBWAY FREAK. She took subways
everywhere. She invented places to go so she would have a
chance to take them. To Orchard Street on the Lower East
Side to shop for bargains, to the Farmers' Market for vegetables fresh with New Jersey dew, to the Battery to see where
Peter Stuyvesant stumped down the gangplank. She took the
GG, the F train, the Brighton express, even the Canarsie line.
Soon she dropped the façade of urgent errands in various parts
of town and spent days underground for the sheer pleasure of
it. She subsisted on orange drinks, Mars Bars, vending machine coffee.

She didn't plan her trips for rush hours, but if the train was
crowded, she got on anyway. She became an expert on where
to place one's hand on the center pole so that it didn't overlap
by a centimeter with anyone else's. She learned to avoid eye
contact and not to breathe too deeply. At night she pored over
subway maps, planning her next day's itinerary.

On Friday evening she was so engrossed in her task that
she let the phone ring at least five times. It was Tom, sounding worried. "Where were you? The phone rang and rang."

"I was in the shower," she lied glibly. "It's so hot here I
shower twice a day."

"It's cool in Geneva. Cool and crisp, with clear blue skies. Just the kind of weather you like."

She waited warily, wondering what he had in mind.

"They want me to stay for another few weeks. There's a man coming in from Oslo that I ought to see."

"So?" She had learned from him how to wait for somebody to get to the point. How to avoid committing yourself or your emotions, until you saw which way the wind was blowing. For her it was an acquired response.

"Laura, why don't you just get on a plane and come over? Especially if it's so hot in New York. You could be here by Sunday night, Monday at the latest, if the weekend's booked."

She was tempted. No graffiti in Switzerland, she knew, no overflowing trash cans. Just clean streets and unambiguous smiles.

Not yet, the subway maps whispered. There are spurs and shuttles and locals you haven't taken yet. There are elevated lines in Queens, secret transfer points in the Bronx.

Again she lied, enjoying her newfound criminal tendencies. "I'm sorry, Tom, I can't. Next weekend is parents' day at the kids' camp, and one of us has to be there." Realizing, as she said it, that it was true. So immersed had she been in her underground adventures that she had blotted out Vermont, as well as Geneva.

"O.K.," he said. "But how are you going to get there?" They seemed always to be having the same conversation. This time her answer was different.

"Don't worry about it. I'll find a way."

"I guess you have to go, but I wish there was a husbands' weekend too." A voice she hadn't heard since their early courting days, soft, sexy, yearning. It made her want to reach out through the telephone wires and touch him.

"I wish there were too," she said. "Do you have to see the Oslo man?"

His tone was brisker now. (They always seemed to synchronize their brief flashes of emotion so that only one of them was feeling strongly at a time.) "Yes, I do, and you have to see the kids." They arranged to speak on Sunday night so she could give him a full report on her weekend at camp.

That night in bed she missed him. For the first time she slept on his side with his pillow pressed against her thighs. Her dreams were full of teasing images. She dreamed that she was riding the rush hour subway. Bodies pressed close against her like old friends, but when she looked up she saw only the blank faces of strangers.

She woke to the rattling of the air-conditioner, which seemed to be shaking itself to pieces. She piled books on top of it and slapped its sides until it calmed down, then wandered out into the airless labyrinth of the apartment. First to Jeffrey's room to see how his hamster was doing. In the dark she could hear Harold running around and around on his wheel. She snapped on the light, and they blinked eyes at each other.

She realized that it had been several days since she had changed the water in his water bottle, and the newspapers on the bottom of his cage. She placed him in a cardboard box while she shredded clean paper into strips and refilled the bottle. She worked quickly, guiltily, as he ran back and forth in the box, making occasional futile attempts to scrabble up the sides. Jeffrey's room looked strange with no clothes on the floor, no half-finished airplane models, no half-eaten apples. As she flipped off the light the wheel began again.

Then Kathy's room, eerie in the glow from the street lamp. Dolls of all nations stared straight ahead on the shelves, stuffed animals crouched on the bed. The room was misleading. Everything in it had been chosen by Kathy in order to make herself seem like the other girls she knew. But the real person was missing.

She resisted the impulse to look through a bureau or desk drawer for clues to her daughter. Eight-year-old girls didn't keep diaries. At least she hadn't when she was eight. But she suspected that what she had or hadn't done as a child would be of little use to her in thinking about Kathy.

Laura tried to remember what her daughter looked like. Jeff's face with his shaggy brows and big straight nose, so much like Tom's, was easy to picture, but the special shape of Kathy's eluded her. And it had only been three weeks.

On to the living room where Jeff and Tom and Kathy's recorders lay sheathed in their cases on top of the piano (she was the only one in the family who wasn't musical). To the dining room to look at the plants they had bought together at the corner plant store. Tonight the apartment was filled with ghosts. She wandered from room to room, feeling like a ghost herself, wondering why she was here, a wife without her husband, a mother without her children.

In the kitchen she made herself a cup of warm cocoa and brought it into the bedroom as if she were bringing it to a sick child. She huddled under the covers, taking small sips until she recovered her equilibrium. It was three o'clock before she fell asleep, on her side of the bed.

She woke at ten to the ringing phone. Her heart leaped as her hand reached for the receiver. It must be Tom calling to say he was coming home, that he didn't care about the man from Oslo, he only wanted to be with her.

But it was Caroline, offering a ride in her air-conditioned car to a crafts fair on East Tenth Street. They arranged to meet in the late afternoon. She looked with surprise at the half-empty cup by her bedside, proof of last night's panic, and the subway maps spread out on the coffee table in the mid-morning sunshine. Today she was no longer compelled to try out every route in the New York City Transit System, but could take the train when she needed to, like everybody else.

The only thing that daylight had not changed was the feeling of sexual longing. For three weeks she had shut off that part of her, like a tidy householder shutting off water and electricity before leaving a summer cottage. Now it had been turned back on by the yearning in Tom's voice. It was not just *Tom's* body she missed; she missed the children's as well. The soft, sweet feel of them as she kissed them good night after their baths, the way they leaned against her in the car when they were coming home late. She realized it had been almost a month since she had touched anyone, if she didn't count the soft brushing of cheeks when she met her women friends, and she didn't.

On the way to the Village Caroline talked nonstop, telling Laura about her son in California (he was painting rocks in the desert on a National Arts Grant), her yoga instructor who was eighteen and very interested in her, the two women who had been raped in the laundry room of her building. All events were given equal weight, calibrated by the fact that they had happened to someone connected with Caroline. Now she was talking about her latest lover, a history professor at NYU whose wife was summering on Martha's Vineyard. "He's there now, the bastard," she said affectionately. "I told him to be careful not to get too sunburned. I've got a couple of new positions I want to try next week."

Laura laughed. "I didn't think there were any new positions," but the conversation made her uncomfortable. At the fair they separated. Caroline wanted to look at the plants — a gestalt therapist, she needed a few more for her office. Laura preferred to wander from booth to booth, as if she were at a bazaar in a foreign country.

She passed tables of leather belts, Moroccan rugs, antique jewelry, and acres of earthenware pots. Her nose was assailed by a spicy mingling of international odors, and she remembered that she had forgotten to have lunch. She was surrounded by delicious possibilities. There were sizzling Italian sausages, sweet and sour spareribs browning on charcoal hibachis, and everywhere the pungent odor of Sabrett sauerkraut. She finally chose a pocket of pita stuffed with fried felafel. The tahini dressing dripped dangerously as she ate. She was munching a large piece of carrot cake, made only of natural ingredients, when Caroline found her.

She had with her a startlingly handsome young man who looked as if he would prefer to be somewhere else. "Laura, see whom I found in the middle of the spider plants." (Caroline was always grammatically correct, even when she was at her most predatory.) Laura stifled the impulse to say "Whom?" as the young man smiled at her. He had evidently taken good care of his teeth.

"Don't I know you?"

"I don't think so. Where . . ."

"At the bus station. Don't your kids go to Camp Tumbleweed?"

Of course. He was the man who had arrived at the very last minute, a duffel bag under one arm and a small redheaded boy under the other. The camp bus had almost left without him. She had noticed how much he looked like his son, the same red hair and bright blue eyes. But when had he had time to notice her? Afterward, when all the parents had stood on the sidewalk, waving and waving, until the bus was out of sight.

"I'm not exactly looking forward to parents' day," he confided. "Sandy always falls apart when I leave, and even though I know he's perfectly happy the minute I'm out of sight, I'm still a wreck." She looked at him with interest. She had never met a man before who talked about his feelings for his child so openly.

"Yes," she said enthusiastically. "My children are the same way."

Caroline watched them both darkly. "Hey, I haven't even introduced you and already you're exchanging intimate confidences. Laura Stone, this is Alan Stevens. Alan used to be a patient of mine."

Laura was still not used to the fact that Caroline seemed to make no distinction between patients and friends. But then Caroline ignored most of the usual rules. Laura, on the other hand, had always obeyed all of them (except, this summer, "Whither thou goest, I go"), and where had it gotten her? To company picnics, and Arbor Day assemblies.

She became aware that Alan was asking her a question.

Would she like to ride with him to the camp next weekend? He was driving up and would appreciate company. She heard herself agreeing, giving him her phone number so that they could make arrangements during the week. It was the brief moment between the falling of dusk and the turning on of the street lights. As she wrote down her number for him, she could barely see.

The people at the booths began to fold their display cases. The purveyors of ethnic foods blew out the flames of their hibachis and packed away their unsold sausages, shish kabobs, teriyaki. (Would they sell it tomorrow, next week, next year, at another fair?) Children clutching helium balloons stamped 10TH ST. CRAFTS FAIR floated toward their homes, where they would crankily refuse to eat their suppers.

Caroline took one of her arms and Alan the other. Together they piloted her through the maze of dispersing craftlovers. Alan murmured, "Excuse me a moment," and disappeared. Soon he was back with a bottle of wine and a silver balloon, which he thrust into Laura's hand. (How did he know it was just what she wanted, but would never have bought for herself?)

It had been many years since she had been in the Village on a summer night. They passed crowds of people dressed as if for some strange costume ball (come as you are, as you were, as you might wish to be) as they searched for a little café that Alan remembered had the best pasta in the Village.

In the park inside Washington Square, old men still played checkers, young men still strummed guitars, but she didn't remember people buying and selling drugs — at least not so openly — in the days when she and Tom used to stroll through the park. Two teen-age boys skated back and forth through the arch, their hips swiveling with the same precision as the ball bearings on their skates. The sound of the disco on their transistor radios almost drowned out the guitars.

In the ladies' room of the at-last-discovered restaurant ("It didn't used to be on McDougal Street," said Alan, surprised), Caroline congratulated her. "You certainly seem to have made an impression. Alan's usually very shy with women. You'll be very good for him."

"But I'm not available," Laura protested. "I'm married. Remember?"

"You may be married, but you're still available. I can tell." Had Caroline been able to see into her bedroom as she lay with her arms around Tom's pillow, or was there a special kind of odor emitted by frustrated females?

The three of them sat close together in a small dark booth, with the balloon hovering above them. In the next room a slightly off-key soprano sang songs about love gone wrong, but they were too far away to hear the words. The wine bottle seemed to be magically unemptiable, or perhaps it had been replaced by another exactly like it. Caroline told outrageously indiscreet anecdotes about her patients. Alan recited Edward Lear as if it were Shakespeare, and asked the waiter for a runcible spoon. They tried to figure out the relationship of the people in the next booth.

It didn't matter what they talked about, or what she ate. She knew only that she was enjoying being somewhere she usually was not, and with people whose every opinion she did not know in advance. Everything any of them said seemed to be either very witty or very profound. What interesting people we are, she thought as she poured herself another glass of wine, and how attractive.

Despite the wine and the fact that the balloon, its helium rapidly depleting, was bobbing against the roof of the car, Caroline drove expertly up Sixth Avenue and on to Broadway. She deposited Alan at Seventy-seventh Street, and Laura in front of her door at two o'clock.

"This was fun," Laura said, retrieving her balloon, her pocketbook, and the two enamel ashtrays she had bought at the fair. "Let's do it again."

To her surprise, Caroline leaned forward across the seats and kissed her warmly on the lips. "Yes, let's," she said, and before Laura could respond in any way she drove off.

As she made her way through the lobby Laura thought sleepily, "Am I then available to everybody?"

∞ *4* ∞

HE WAS DREAMING that they were making love on a giant water bed. It was marvelous, satisfying, gymnastic, better than it had ever been in real life. He was awakened by the insistent ringing of the phone. Groggy, he reached for the receiver, expecting to hear Laura's voice telling him that parents' day had been canceled, or that she had decided "to hell with parenthood" and was coming anyway.

Instead, the hotel operator. Seven o'clock, and she hoped he had had a good night's rest. He rose reluctantly. As he showered and soaped, the dream lingered. Strange to have erotic dreams about one's own wife. Almost indecent. Hypothesis to be explored: Men seldom have fantasies about the women they live with. He didn't know much about other men's fantasies. Only his own, comfortable and comforting, like leering old teddy bears.

Time to button and zip himself into his summer weight business suit, cram the appropriate papers into his briefcase, and disguise himself as a respectable citizen. By the time he had finished, the dream was gone.

It returned at lunch, as he sat sipping wine from the carafe that appeared automatically at every meal, as if deposited by a wine-pushing genie. At two the terrace of the hotel was still filled with leisurely lunchers, enjoying the good food and the splendid view of the lake. Many of the men had been joined by their wives. An air of relaxation today, in contrast to the intense conferring of the last three weeks. The pressure to appear competent, knowledgeable, busy, easing up at last.

He felt conspicuous sitting at a table all by himself. An odd man out. Why had Laura refused to come with him? Didn't she realize how unsettled he would be without her?

He had always liked Geneva. The way the Swiss managed to keep themselves and their city clean, attractive, and calm. But now, without Laura and with the conference over, it seemed sterile, even stuffy. A lonely place with nothing to do.

She had never rejected him before. Now she had rejected him not once, but twice. First when she had inexplicably announced that she wanted to spend July by herself in the city. The second time last night. She might at least have had the decency to pretend to be disappointed about not coming. She had sounded positively delighted.

What was happening to her in New York that made leaving it so unappealing? Suspicion in the glass along with the wine. Maybe she had a lover. Maybe she was paying him back for Amy.

But no. That couldn't be. She didn't know about Amy. But wait a minute, what was it she had said when they had been arguing about the summer — something about its being her turn? Could she have meant her turn to have an affair?

Pictures began to form in his mind. Laura in a café, Laura on the phone, Laura in bed with her lover. No, that was ridiculous. Laura was not secretive. If she had known about Amy she would have said something. She would have cried, asking how he could have done such a thing to her, to their marriage, to their children. Yes, she would surely have brought in the children, as if his siring of them had been his only important contribution. It was true — as soon as the children were born, she had begun to lose interest in him. Perhaps she would have preferred a fish father, one who fertilizes his potential offspring, then keeps on swimming.

It had not always been like that. Not in the beginning. Memories now of the summer they were first married, before there were any children. They had been like two children themselves, testing the previously forbidden contents of the cooky jar. Totally absorbed in each other, the two most delightful people on earth.

When they were on their honeymoon, her mother had sent a heavy fisherman's sweater, writing, "It is sometimes very cold on Cape Ann in June." Giggling as she read her married name, "Mrs. Thomas Stone," Laura asked wonderingly, "How did I get a man's name?"

They stayed in their room until noon, emerging from the inn only for huge meals of steak and lobster. Long walks on the beach, filling their pockets with pebbles and shells, their shoes with sand. He outlined his theory on the eventual triumph of science over the humanities. She explained to him why Emily Dickinson was a better poet than Edna St. Vincent Millay.

Of course all was not pleasure and delight. Since they were both almost totally inexperienced, several lovemaking sessions had ended with frustration on his part, tears on hers. But somehow their difficulties in making love had not affected their closeness. They held each other tight and assured each other that it would be better as soon as they had more practice. Of course it was. They had taught each other, and they had both been eager students. The surprising discovery that making love was something you had to learn how to do, like any other skill.

Honeymoon memories were abruptly interrupted by George Stockton, leaning his well-tailored bulk against the small wrought iron table. "Tom, I'd like a copy of that paper you gave yesterday. It was first rate." A compliment from George was rare, and Tom was pleased. There was always the possibility that he had delivered a paper of complete nonsense, intelligible only to him.

George was in no hurry to leave. In fact seemed positively eager to stay and chat. Tom invited him to sit down and join him for a post-luncheon cognac. He lowered himself into a chair, which creaked under his weight.

"What are your plans now, Tom? No more real meetings, thank God."

He realized that he had no plans, that he had not thought beyond this morning's final session, and the time sometime next week when Mr. Torval would be arriving from Norway. Not waiting for an answer, George leaned forward, his belly straining against the expensive material of his shirt. "I've been meaning to ask you, Tom. Where's Laura this year?" He lowered his voice confidentially. "Everything all right at home?"

"Oh, everything's fine," he lied. "She had some dental work she needed to get over with. Otherwise she'd be here."

Had he protested too much? Also, why hadn't he told George the real reason? Maybe because it was none of George's business. Or maybe because he didn't know the real reason. Definitely something different in her voice last night, something not connected with him. How could he be so sure he knew what Laura would or wouldn't do? Perhaps that was why he had placed her in a month-long dental session.

George was looking at him with a bemused smile. Could he read his thoughts? "Coming to the fête tonight? I hear it's going to be pretty wild, at least for the Swiss."

A sudden strong desire to get away, before George popped a button and his hairy navel emerged. He rose, glancing at his watch, pretending that he had just remembered an appointment.

Back in the room he read about the Fête de Genève in the brochure that came with the conference material. A trilingual festival. People coming from all the cantons to celebrate with singing, dancing, drinking. Maybe he would go. It was time for a little post-conference carousing. Laura was not the only one entitled to time off for good behavior.

When he left the hotel in the early evening, the city had been transformed. Ordinary streets had become bowers, with crepe paper and roses strung between the trees. He could hear music everywhere — accordions, flutes, drums, even (unaccountably) bagpipes skirling faintly in the distance. Groups of people danced through the streets throwing confetti at each other. Many were wearing costumes (he couldn't tell whether French, Italian, or German), the men in felt vests and knee socks with tassels, the women in embroidered blouses and bright shawls. For a while he was content to watch from the sidelines, feeling like a sparrow in a city of peacocks. Then Suzanne, a young Swiss girl who worked at the hotel, called to him. "Professor Stone, come and join the fête."

He had noticed her in the dining room of the hotel. She had a teasing, impish look that he liked. Tonight she was wearing a full-skirted dress of red and yellow, with a flower placed between her breasts. He grabbed her outstretched hand and let himself be pulled into the street. Behind them a brass band blared out a march. Ahead Swiss bells were ringing. Before he knew what he was doing, he had become a marcher.

Holding Suzanne's warm hand in his, he marched past the hotel, past the banks, the embassies, the buildings that housed the huge staffs of worthy international organizations. People leaned precariously out of windows, throwing shredded memos and annual reports. Bits of colored paper covered his shoulders, his hair. They crept into his pockets and crunched underneath his socks.

Dogs and cats with collars made of flowers were held aloft by their owners. A huge St. Bernard trotted along beside them for several blocks. It sniffed at their heels, and almost seemed to march to the music. Maybe it was really a man wearing a dog suit. Tom was no longer absolutely sure of his perceptions. Was that George grinning at him from the sidewalk? He strode past, holding Suzanne's hand, now almost like an extension of his own, not looking closely enough to be certain.

"I'm hungry," she said suddenly. "Let us get something to eat. Do you like fondu?"

Suzanne was surprised that he had not yet tasted it. "We'll have to get some for you tonight. You can't leave Geneva without having tasted Swiss fondu."

She led him by the hand, as if she were a parent taking a favored child for a special treat. She showed him how to spear a piece of bread on the long-handled fork, to immerse it in the bubbling mix of melted cheese and wine, to hold it up for a minute while the extra liquid dripped off, and then to plunge the morsel into his mouth. One of the few foods that tasted even better than it looked.

He had no idea he was so hungry. He hadn't eaten since lunch, and that had been mostly wine and cognac. Suzanne watched him with amusement. Then she pushed his hand aside. "Excuse me, Professor, leave a little for me." Did she call him "professor" out of respect (after all he was entitled to it; he did give seminars on industrial chemistry at the university each spring) or as a way of teasing him? Whichever it was, he liked it.

As they ate, she asked him to tell her about life in New York. "It must be a wonderful place to live," she said, "not boring and stuffy, like Geneva." When she sighed, her whole bosom sighed. Amazing breasts. He wondered if she was aware of how they looked as she leaned over the fondu.

"Geneva's not stuffy tonight."

"But what about the other nights?" she said plaintively. "Tell me about the lights in Times Square. Are there really neon signs as tall as a ten-story building?"

Times Square with its peepshows, porn bookstores, weaving drunks and addicts. He remembered the last time he had boarded a subway in Times Square. A short, bald-headed, muscular man wearing a karate robe had sat with a board suspended across his knees, demonstrating karate chops. He let out a startling grunt each time his bare fist hit the wood. He did not seem to be violent, merely demonstrating his skill, but people had begun to edge away to the other end of the car. An old woman, wearing three sweaters and at least two coats, was having an intense argument with an invisible person whom she called Fred.

The New York City he knew couldn't possibly compete with the New York in Suzanne's head. He tried not to disturb her fantasy city too much. He liked the intent, serious way she asked him questions, as if anything he said, on any subject, was interesting to her. She had a way of making him feel both old and young at the same time. A scholar and a rake combined.

He had felt this way with Amy. At least he had at first. What a pleasure it had been to have a woman's undivided attention. A woman who wasn't mentally making grocery lists, or wondering if the children were dressed warmly enough. Amy had really listened, asked him detailed questions about his work in the lab as if she cared. And of course, working for the same company, she had understood what he was doing, how complex it was, how often unrewarding. She had understood his frustration in trying to verify test results, in getting his scientific papers published.

Only one aspect of his life Amy had not understood. The ties that bound him to his family, to his children, to Laura. Her own family lived in California and she seldom saw them. She said she didn't miss them, that people were better off without families, except maybe at Thanksgiving and Christmas (there had been no problem for them, they had not lasted until Thanksgiving). She was not torn as he had been torn. He had somehow thought he could have both her *and* his family, or to be more honest, he hadn't thought. He had just needed her very much that summer (the ninth year of his marriage), and when she started to need him in return, he had fled.

As he had decided it was time to flee from Suzanne now. She was looking at him expectantly, inquiringly. Now, seeing her for the first time as a person, not just a friendly hand pulling him into the fête, or an attractive body, he saw how very young she was. Much younger than Amy.

"How old are you, Suzanne? I want the truth."

She pouted. "Eighteen on my last birthday."

More likely on her next. She was not many years older than Kathy. But Kathy would never pursue an older man so shamelessly. Untrue. At three she used to climb up on his lap, snuggle against him with such trust that he thought his heart would melt. Even at eight she dashed forward to give him a hug as soon as he walked in the door. And she still climbed into his lap when he read to her, though the time was coming soon when she would be too big for this. Had come already, perhaps, although neither of them was willing to acknowledge it. He had been unfaithful to Laura with so many women. Mostly in his thoughts, it's true, but it was a distinction that he was no longer sure mattered. In any case, it was time to take Suzanne home. Doubtless her mother was waiting up for her. Or possibly her father.

She didn't seem surprised. Perhaps she too had had enough adventure for one night. On the way home he bought her a red silk kerchief from a man who was stowing them away in his pockets like a nervous magician. The fête was almost over, most of the revelers asleep in their neat Swiss beds. Only a few sleepy couples shuffled through the confetti.

Suzanne's house looked like the ones that came with Jeff's train set. Dormer roof, geraniums in the window boxes. He had a sudden urge to show her a picture of Laura and the children. She peered closely at the photograph. He realized that she was probably nearsighted. The intense expressive gaze that he had taken for adoration might very well be myopia.

Suzanne handed the picture back to him. "Your wife looks very intelligent." She showed him a picture of her fiancé, a tall unsmiling young man in the uniform of the Swiss Guards. He told her that he looked very brave.

Before leaving, she kissed him lightly on the lips. "Pleasant dreams, Professor." He held her to him for a moment, enjoying the warmth of her body, and wondering if anything more was expected of him. She giggled and gently disengaged herself, whispering, "I think you have fondu in your mustache."

It was a long time before he could fall asleep. The lights from the café across the street shone directly into the room. The floor was strewn with a trail of confetti that had showered from his clothes as he took them off. Like the trail of bread crumbs left by Hansel and Gretel when they had been led into the woods and abandoned by their parents.

Lying in bed, he thought how much his children would have loved the fête. (Laura would probably have disapproved, considering it too disorganized, too noisy.) When he had taken them to the circus last spring Kathy had squealed with delight at the mountain of pink cotton candy he bought her, held his hand tight when the man was shot out of a cannon.

Suddenly he wondered if the children were all right, if anything had happened at the camp that nobody had told him about. He had only had one postcard from each, obviously written under a counselor's close supervision. That they were too busy to write, he had seen as a good sign. Now he wasn't so sure. Anyway, he wanted to hear their voices. He was their father. He didn't have to have a reason.

He stumbled toward the closet in the dark, looking for the pen in his jacket pocket. He calculated the time difference between Geneva and Vermont, hoping he was getting it right, and picked up the phone.

∞ *5* ∞

O N Tuesday afternoon Lydia called to say that half the paintings in the show had been sold already. Also that she was working on a giant painting tentatively called *Rockets over New Jersey*. It was eleven feet by eight — the biggest so far — she would call Laura when it was finished.

Caroline called to say that Barbara and Michael were seeing lawyers. Also that her professor had decided to stay in Martha's Vineyard for the summer. She was furious, but luckily the yoga instructor was still in town. He was teaching her positions that even her professor didn't know. Had Laura ever tried it in the lotus position? And would she like to go to a concert of early Renaissance music?

Laura answered no to both questions. She might have enjoyed the concert, but she suspected that Caroline only wanted an audience. She was feeling restless enough these days without being forced to listen, between madrigals, to the intimate details of Caroline's latest sexual adventures.

Instead she went for a walk alone along Riverside Drive, looking at the buildings and people as if she were seeing them for the first time. In some sense, of course, she was. She usually had the children with her, or gazed distractedly from the windows of the bus, while planning her errands in mid-town.

Today she looked at the gargoyles, the ornamental balus-trades, and the octagonal rooms nestled between Art Deco apartment houses. She half expected to see Rapunzel's long golden hair descending from one of the tower windows.

Once she saw the small face of a monkey pressed against the window guards of a first-floor room. Next door someone thrust a bony hand through a space in an iron grate and watered dusty geraniums. The voice of a frantically amateur soprano soared out of a third-floor apartment.

Across the street, under the trees, meticulously dressed old people with paid companions in white shoes, dozed. Unhappy young women wrote in their journals, and thirsty alcoholics sipped from bottles in brown bags. One old man looked as if he were waiting for a chance to open his raincoat for the next child who came by. She walked past them all, trying not to stare, feeling like a visitor from another planet.

On Tuesday, sometime between three and four o'clock in the morning, two disastrous things happened simultaneously. The air-conditioner stopped working, and one of Laura's right molars began to ache. She woke bathed in sweat, aware of a small but persistent pain in her jaw. She had been so busy shepherding the children to dentists and doctors before they left for camp, and nagging Tom about his annual check-up, that she had forgotten about her own.

It was not possible to sleep in Jeff's room, with the sound of Harold on his nightly treadmill. She moved to Kathy's and discovered she couldn't open the window. It had been painted almost shut two years ago, and Kathy had never ob-jected. She liked to keep the room as close to hothouse tem-perature as possible. Unlike her mother, she seemed to flourish in the heat.

In the morning Laura called the dentist and the air-condi-tioner service, telling each it was an emergency. The dentist agreed to see her that morning; the air-conditioner people said they would try to send a man the next day.

"Just a little cavity," said Dr. Cavanaugh. "I'll fill it as soon as the anesthesia takes effect. And how is your husband? Is his bridge holding up?" She had never liked Dr. Cavanaugh, but Tom said he was the best dentist in town and that one didn't go to dentists for their personalities. She told him that she couldn't report on Tom's bridgework, since he was in Geneva.

"Oh?" said Dr. Cavanaugh, looking intently into her open mouth. "And you're in the city by yourself?"

At first she thought she was imagining it. It seemed so unlikely that she could be feeling what she thought she was feeling. His starched white stomach pressed against her side as he chiseled, his arm lingering on her arm as he probed. Usually, while she was having a tooth filled she practiced what she still remembered from a yoga class she had taken just after Jeff was born, willing herself mindless, or at least elsewhere; but the feeling that the human being next to her was closer than he needed to be for what he was doing was unavoidable.

She was completely at his mercy, with the drill poised above her as she lay supine on his dentist space couch. She considered biting his soft white fingers, but decided that might only enrage him. At last he said the words she had been waiting to hear, "You can spit now," and she was released. She sat up, feeling slightly dizzy.

"There, that wasn't so bad was it?" he asked, beaming with dental pride. "By the way," he added, pausing in the doorway, "doesn't it get lonesome for you in the city by yourself?"

"No," she replied crisply, scooping up her pocketbook and pushing past him, "it doesn't." She went directly from his office, as she almost always did, to Bloomingdale's, where she bought *marrons glacés* and goose liver pâté, as if to prove that she was not the kind of woman who got her kicks from being leaned on by a dentist.

In front of Bloomingdale's a girl and a boy were playing Vivaldi on a violin and a flute. She bought a giant chocolate chip cookie from a cookie truck parked next to the curb, and dropped her change into the derby on the sidewalk in front of the musicians. The cookie was delicious, the music was delightful, and her tooth had finally stopped hurting. In many ways, she thought, New York is the only civilized place to live.

Late the next morning, the muscular young air-conditioner repair man was as obvious as the dentist. "Nothing wrong with this machine, lady, except old age. What you need is a new model, one with more power." Or was she just reading double meanings into everything these days?

Laura retreated to Riverside Park, feeling that she would surely be safe with the mothers and the little children. Very little had changed since she had last pushed Kathy's stroller down the steep hill to the playground. She had read about mothers organizing themselves into committees to hound their city councilmen, and when that failed, cleaning up the area themselves. It was less littered with broken glass and trash than it used to be. But there were still toddlers fighting over toys in the sandbox, older children perched perilously on the top bars of the Jungle gym or sliding down backward on the slides, little ones calling, "Push me, Mommy, push me," on the swings. In the middle of the playground, children in bathing suits and shorts ran in and out of the sprinkler's spray, splashing and screaming. She sat down on a bench near the gate and opened her book.

How strange to be here without a child. She felt almost as if the mothers might turn on her and order her out of the park. No one glanced in her direction. The women were too busy talking to each other, while their eyes followed their darting children as they moved from one piece of potentially injurious equipment to another. Occasionally a squalling child emerged from the park with a wounded knee, and howled for its mother.

She remembered the first time she and Tom had come to

the park as parents. The babies in the other carriages had seemed huge misshapen monsters, compared to the perfection of their small sleeping son. They had sat on the bench to rest (Jeff was still waking almost every three hours), tired but feeling smug and pleased with themselves. They too had accomplished the miracle. They had produced a child, and thus had a legitimate passport to the playground.

After that, of course, it had been mostly she alone who had come to the park, although sometimes Tom would join her on weekends. More often, though, as the children grew older, he would take them off on a special expedition, to the Statue of Liberty or the Bronx Zoo, while she luxuriated in the sinful pleasure of a Sunday nap or a chance to read the *Times* without interruption.

The park was *her* bailiwick on weekdays. She was in full charge of catastrophes — scraped knees, lost balls, the half-eaten Popsicle that slid down the stick and into the sandbox, the child, usually Kathy, who had to go to the bathroom as soon as they crossed the street to the park. She always brought a book with her, along with the pails, dump trucks, boxes of raisins, and Handiwipes, but she almost never read it. The plot of most novels suffered when one had to glance up after each paragraph.

Today, though, she was free to read whole chapters in peace. Instead she chose to look at other people's children, and to eavesdrop on the women around her.

One had a friend who had been to *est* and felt that it had changed her life. Another was looking for a baby sitter so that she and her husband could go to an Arica session for the weekend. "Joe says it's the only way he can get to see me without the kids around."

Another young woman giggled. "They *do* pick the damndest times. Once when we were just about to . . . " She lowered her voice, and heads clustered around her in order not to miss a word. Yes, Laura thought, life in the playground had

changed. Just a few years ago, the talk had been of breast-
feeding, toilet training, sibling rivalry. No women she knew
ever talked about their sex lives, although it was obvious from
their strollers and carriages and bulging bellies that they had
all had some.

She returned to her book, but her mind drifted. Had Tom
ever felt the children coming between them? She didn't think
so. She had tried very hard to make him feel included, not by
asking his advice on the daily crises of child rearing (that after
all was her department), but by telling him the special things
they had said and done. They literally jumped into his arms
when he opened the door each evening. Often she held herself
back, so that the children could have their special pre-supper
time with their father.

The heads on the next bench had separated. The conversation seemed to have ended when someone said enviously,
"Well, at least you have something to interrupt." The others
were silent, as if her words might be contagious if they
responded.

She could hear the sound of the Good Humor Man's bell,
still distant, but approaching. As always, he managed to arrive
at the playground just before it was time to start back. Already
the children were dropping from the Jungle gym, tumbling
off the slide and the seesaw to tug at their mothers' jeans and
plead for a Fudgsicle.

A memory tugged at the edge of Laura's thoughts: the summer
three years ago when she had sat in this playground every
afternoon in July, staying even after most of the other mothers
had left to trudge up the hill to supper in apartments on Riverside Drive and West End. Afraid to leave the park, to sit in
her own apartment wondering when Tom was going to come
home. It seemed to her he came later each night, mumbling

something about extra work at the office, while the children cried, "Daddy, where *were* you? We waited and waited."

After a while Kathy and Jeff stopped asking. They seemed to accept her explanation that Daddy was extra busy these days. She turned on the TV set, something she had never done before, something she disapproved of as a way of solving problems, or even of filling silences. They immersed themselves in the adventures of Mighty Mouse, were soothed by the soft voice of Mr. Rogers.

She stayed in the kitchen, chopping vegetables, trying not to listen for the sound of the key in the lock. She never questioned him about what kept him away from her and the children so many evenings, and why he was so distracted when he did come home. She just sat tight and hugged the children, and tried not to think about what might be happening to him, to them.

One evening, drawn by the soothing sound of Mr. Rogers's voice saying how it was all right to be scared, everybody was scared, she came out of the kitchen and joined the children on the couch. It soon became a ritual, her watching Mr. Rogers with the children. They would call her from the other room, "Mommy, your program's on," and she would sit with them and watch as Mr. Rogers put on his cardigan and slippers, and told them he was glad to be with them.

Sometimes the children grew restless and wandered off to their bedrooms, or started to squabble over a board game, but she always stayed, as if enchanted. Once when Mr. Rogers said that everybody needed somebody to love and to love them back, she burst into tears, startling herself and the children. That was the night she took them up the block at seven o'clock to the pizza parlor, not able to stay in the apartment for another minute.

Each night, in their sweltering bedroom (they had not yet bought an air-conditioner) she lay awake, yearning for sleep and forgetfulness, acutely aware of the man sleeping beside her. She was tired all that summer. The nights of not sleeping, the days of not thinking, not noticing, using all her energy not to feel.

Once she had awakened to find Tom's half of the bed empty. He was in the living room watching television. "Too hot to sleep," he had said apologetically.

They sat next to each other, not touching, staring straight ahead until four o'clock in the morning, watching Ingrid Bergman leaving Leslie Howard in *Intermezzo*. She had wanted so much to move closer to him, to ask him to put his arms around her and keep her safe, but she couldn't. Safe from what, from whom?

When the movie was over they returned to their bed together. Just as she was falling asleep, Tom began to make love to her in a harsh, impersonal way. No kisses, no words, only direct sexual motions. Her spirit was repelled, but her body responded. When it was over, Tom fell asleep almost instantly. She lay awake until morning, feeling used, abused, more alone than before. Yet they had acted together. It had not been against her will.

One afternoon toward the end of August, Tom had unexpectedly appeared in the playground, just as she was starting to gather the sand buckets and the shovels. He carried a rose, which he thrust at her without a word. She was so surprised that she dropped Jeffrey's dump truck to clutch at the flower. The children, who had been taking their last frantic slides of the day, called out, "Daddy, swing us, swing us." He placed each child on a swing and took turns pushing them back and forth until at last even they had had enough. Then the three of them had climbed the hill together, a child clinging to each hand, while she straggled behind, the straw satchel full of toys in one hand, the rose in the other. After that day Tom began to come home earlier.

In the fall she had not come back to the playground. The children were growing too old for it. They preferred the one a few blocks farther down the Drive where they could climb on huge rocks, and Jeff could play ball with his friends.

∽∽∽

The Good Humor Man was now at the very gate of the playground. Out of the corner of her eye she saw a small child, barely able to walk, moving away from her mother, past the Jungle gym, toward the sound of the ringing bell. It was surprising that something that small and unsteady could move so fast. Fortunately Laura's maternal reflexes were still good. In a second she was up and running, scooping up the startled toddler seconds before she would have crashed into the wagon of the oblivious ice cream man.

"Lady," he said self-righteously, "you ought to watch your kid. I almost ran it down."

"She's not my child," she said. At the same moment the child realized the same fact and began to howl desperately for her mother. Laura continued to hold on to the sticky hand until an anxious-faced woman emerged from the far end of the playground.

"Thanks," she said to Laura. "I was watching my other two and this one got away." She smacked the child across her diapered bottom. "Haven't I told you not to run away from me, you naughty girl?" Mother and sobbing daughter, plus two grubby sons, left the playground together.

Laura bought a coconut-covered Creamsicle from the Good Humor Man to show him that she didn't blame him, and realized what she ought to have remembered, that Creamsicles never taste as good as they look.

Later that night, while filling Harold's food dish with sunflower seeds and birdseed, she had a feeling of unease. Perhaps the incident in the playground had been a sign. Maybe one of her children was in danger. Maybe something had happened at the camp and they had been trying to get her all afternoon while she had been sitting in the park.

Camp Tumbleweed had a strict rule against calling any

time except between four and six on Sunday afternoons, but suddenly Laura had an overwhelming need to talk to her children, to hear their voices, and to know for sure that they were all right.

At eight o'clock she could stand it no longer and dialed the number of the camp. The phone rang for a long time. A firm no-nonsense voice informed her that all campers were at evening campfire and could not be disturbed. "Unless," said the voice, showing its first flickering sign of humanity, "it's an emergency."

"Yes," she said. "It's an emergency." Instantly Laura regretted her words, but the owner of the voice had already left the phone to go in search of Jeff. Like his mother, he was a worrier. He would worry all the way from the lake to the camp office where the phone was. He would think that something terrible had happened to her or to Tom.

After what seemed a very long time (had the campsite expanded since she visited it last summer?) she heard Jeff's voice, breathless and concerned. "Hey Mom, what's the matter? Why are you calling?"

She breathed a sigh of relief. "I just wanted to know how you were. I hadn't heard from you for a long time."

"I wrote you a letter today," he said defensively. "I'm pretty busy here, you know."

"I know. How is Kathy? Is she all right?"

Now he sounded annoyed. "Of course she's all right. She's fine. What's the matter with you two anyway?" He told her that Tom had called the night before, pulling him out of the weekly talent show just as he was about to play the recorder.

"Your father called from Switzerland?"

"Yup." Jeff did not appear to find this as extraordinary as she did. "Hey Mom, are you coming up this weekend?"

She assured him that she would see him and Kathy in a few days. Someone yelled at Jeff to get off the phone, the director needed to make a call, and before she could say good-bye, he was gone.

She felt shaken by his revelation that Tom had called from Geneva. Perhaps she had been worrying about the wrong members of the family.

She began to think about how she had spent her time since the day she and Tom had parted at the airport. Her freedom had consisted almost entirely of tasks omitted — meals not cooked, missing sneakers and library cards not searched for, lists not made.

When she came back from the weekend, she would try something more adventurous. Scuba diving at the Y, or African dance at the Clark Center. She might even learn to drive. Then she could go places by herself, not have to wait for someone to drive her. Anyway, something new. Something to show for her solo summer.

As she drifted off to sleep at last, the phone rang. It was Alan, eager and apologetic. "I meant to call you earlier this week, but I got sidetracked." He didn't say by what. He said he would pick her up at eight on Saturday morning. "I'll call just before I leave so you can be downstairs waiting for me." She liked his voice over the telephone. He managed to sound both intimate and efficient at the same time.

"It'll be good to have a chance to talk," he said, and added teasingly, "I've got a few surprises for you." She told him she would be ready.

∽ 6 ∽

THE FIRST SURPRISE was that Alan didn't appear until nine. When he arrived, he didn't say anything about the time, so neither did she. She had spent the past hour pacing through the apartment, checking the windows, the pilot light of the stove, the back door, all the ritual acts she was used to performing before leaving on a trip, however brief, while Tom waited impatiently in the car with his mental meter running.

She found that she was very glad to see him, whatever the time. He looked even younger than she had remembered. He opened the car door for her, something Tom had long ago stopped doing, and bowed slightly, ushering her into his orange BMW. In a T-shirt and tight jeans he seemed more like a junior counselor than a parent. The back seat was stuffed with cookies and candies he was bringing to Sandy, plus an outsize rubber giraffe. She tucked her small package for Kathy and Jeff into a corner near the window, and they were off.

Weaving in and out between more cautious vehicles on the West Side Highway, they crossed the George Washington Bridge and went speeding on their way north. If Tom had driven the way Alan did, she would have been terrified. Some-

how with Alan she was not. She had not really expected him
to drive any other way. Indeed, she felt, as she looked at his
face, so relaxed and intent at the same time, that he probably
didn't realize there *was* another way to drive.

She took off her scarf and let the wind blow through her
hair. It was a clear sunny day — as Tom had said about Geneva, just the kind of weather she liked. She wondered why
she had waited so long to leave the city. Nothing had kept
her there, after all, with the smog and the soot and piles of
rotting garbage, except habit. And it had taken a visit to camp
to get her to move. It was all right to get into a car with a
strange man, if you were going to visit your children.

"What are you smiling at?" Alan asked. "It is a private
joke?"

"Not really. It just feels good to be in a car and going
somewhere."

"Sandy and I go exploring every weekend. He's crazy about
cars."

She pictured the small child she had seen under Alan's
arm, bouncing about in the front seat, or with his head stuck
far out the window yelling, "Faster, Dad. Drive faster." She
realized suddenly why she had not had her usual struggle
with the seat belt. In this car there were none.

Had them taken out, Alan said. He never used his, and
Sandy wouldn't keep his buckled. Would she like a pear? He
thought there was one in the glove compartment that should
be just about ripe by now.

There was, along with a crumpled package of Kleenex, a
map of New England, and ten parking tickets. They shared
the pear, passing it back and forth while Laura wondered
where Sandy's mother was, and how she could find out tact-
fully. Tact, it turned out, was not necessary. Alan was eager
to talk about himself.

He told her about his job writing copy for an advertising
agency, his attempts to find a substitute mother for Sandy.

"It's hard to go up to a woman you're dating and say, 'Would you like to take care of my little boy?' " he said ruefully. About the novel he was writing evenings after Sandy went to bed. (Is everybody in the United States writing a novel? she wondered. There were clearly more writers than readers.)

His ex-wife had run off to California with her primal scream therapist when Sandy was two. Now she was leading a nude encounter group, strictly asexual, she claimed. Probably true, said Alan — she had never been very much interested in sex. Recently she had started sending him letters saying she wanted Sandy back. He didn't think California was a good place to bring up a child, especially with the earthquakes and the San Andreas Fault. Sandy would probably like the therapy groups though. He'd always liked taking off his clothes and yelling.

"Enough about me," he said at last. "Let's pull over to the next grassy knoll and have a picnic lunch, while I try to figure out where we are." It had never occurred to her he didn't know. Tom always marked out the route in advance, or, if they were going to a place they hadn't been before, ordered a Triptik from the Triple A. Although she had always done poorly in school in what they called map skills, she had learned to read the Triptik, which showed only a small section of the route at a time.

Alan spread a checkered tablecloth on the grass and produced a delightful lunch of cold chicken, white wine, cheese, and fruit. He had even brought crystal glasses. It was just the kind of elegant picnic she had always imagined having. Alan was an attentive and thoughtful host. He spread out a rug for her to sit on, offered her black olives and stuffed grape leaves, poured wine into her glass, and waited for her approval. Very different from the picnics with the children — undercooked hamburgers on a smoky grill and squashed peanut butter and jelly sandwiches.

She felt flattered, excited, a little like the woman in the Manet painting, except that she had her clothes on. Alan seemed to have forgotten that they were in the country for any other reason than to sit in this shaded glen. It *was* the perfect spot for a picnic — there was even a tree to lean against and a murmuring brook to keep the wine cool. He smiled blissfully and suggested that they take off their shoes and go wading. He made her a daisy crown and placed it gently on her head, telling her that she didn't look old enough to be the mother of two school-age children.

Unfortunately, she kept remembering that he had said they were lost, and that she *was* the mother of two children who were expecting them by midafternoon for the gymnastics exhibition. At last she could restrain herself no longer.

"Alan, don't you think we should look at the map? The children will be waiting."

He seemed surprised at her intensity. "Yes, of course," he said. "I have no objections."

Luckily, she had noticed the name of the last town they had passed through. They seemed to be on a side road running parallel to the highway. If they continued in the direction they were going, they could rejoin it in about five miles. While she pored over the route, pleased with her newfound skills, Alan repacked the picnic basket. "Did you like my surprise?" he asked, as she struggled to refold the map.

She stopped, remembering the many times she had prepared special surprises for Tom or the children; how deeply disappointed she had often been when they didn't notice. "Yes, it was lovely, just the kind of picnic I've always wanted," she said, trying to sound appreciative and sincere. "But now," and here she sounded so much like Tom that she was amazed, "it really is time for us to be on our way."

Back in the car Alan was silent, apparently feeling that she had been insufficiently impressed. She decided to ignore his need for praise. Instead, she concentrated on the map, calling out route numbers and turns like a combination drill sergeant and subway conductor. They arrived at the camp at five o'clock, exactly forty-five minutes after the gymnastic exhibition had begun.

Jeff was waiting for them at the entrance, his tender young ankles visible below his too-short jeans. (Had they shrunk in the camp laundry, or had he grown that much in a month?) He ran up to the car and opened the door almost before it stopped. He gave Alan a brief confused glance. "Hey, whose car *is* this?" Before she could answer, he grabbed her hand and pulled her out. "Hurry, Mom. Kathy's going on any minute." He looked as if he were about to cry with desperation.

She allowed herself to be pulled down the pebble-strewn path. Through the thin soles of her sandals the pebbles felt like boulders. She wished she had worn sneakers as she had planned. Had she wanted to impress Alan with her slender sandaled feet? Out of the corner of her eye she was aware of him stumbling behind her, but there was no time to wait. They arrived at the tent, filled with perspiring, anxious parents, just as the camp director, Uncle Manny, was introducing Kathy's group, advanced acrobatics.

It was a few minutes before she was able to catch her breath and focus clearly enough on the stage to pick out her small tumbling daughter from the mass of performing arms and legs. When she did, she was astonished. She had never imagined that dreamy Kathy, so unaware of others, was capable of such precision. She never missed a beat or a movement. Then the director announced a special solo, performed and choreographed by Kathy Stone.

Her daughter's arms and legs almost disappeared in a blur as she turned cartwheels from one end of the stage to the other, ending triumphantly on her feet, not even seeming to be out of breath. The audience rose to its feet and clapped. She said to the woman next to her, "That's my daughter." The woman smiled. "She seems very talented."

Laura settled back into her seat, still marveling. How could *her* daughter be so graceful, so effortlessly coordinated, when she herself had always been so uncoordinated? She had never learned to ride a bike; when she had been forced to go ice skating as a child, her ankles had buckled almost to the ice.

A small figure nuzzled against her side. "Hi, Mommy. Did you see me?"

"Yes I saw you. You were wonderful." She resisted the impulse to pull Kathy into her lap, and hugged her instead. "I didn't know you could do things like that."

Kathy shrugged. "I've been practicing. See you later." Then she was gone.

Jeff and Kathy joined her for the parents' banquet in the dining hall. She began to see why they complained so much about the food. It was hard to believe it had been upgraded for parental consumption. The meal consisted of gray mashed potatoes with lumps, rubbery fried chicken, and limp lettuce leaves. The dessert, chocolate cake, was greeted with cheers. She saw Sandy and Alan on the other side of the dining room and waved.

Both her children looked tanned and fit. They seemed to be managing so admirably without her that she felt a twinge. Was her mothering stint to be over so soon? They talked with their mouths full and their elbows on the table, but for once she didn't mind. She was glad to see them and to hear everything they had to say. When they dragged her to their cabins to introduce her to their counselors and their friends, she allowed herself to be pulled, responding to all requests. It was a pleasure to be needed, not to have to make her own decisions for a while.

In Kathy's cabin a large pleasant-faced woman was carefully inspecting her daughter's rock collection. Kathy pushed her mother toward the absorbed couple. "Sarah, this is my mother."

Sarah looked up and grinned. "And this is mine. Did you see the rock I found this morning? My mother says it's a fossil."

The woman smiled. "I said it *might* be, Sarah. I'll have to take it back to the museum and check for sure." She put out a large, capable hand. "I'm Enid Sims."

A familiar name. Where had she read it? Suddenly Alan burst into the cabin, causing a little girl in the corner who was changing from shorts to jeans to let out a shriek. "There you are," he said. "I've been looking for you everywhere."

Now she remembered. An article in the Sunday *Times* — intriguing remnants of early man discovered in Kenya. Enid Sims had been in charge of the expedition.

Alan grabbed Laura's hand, determined that she would not elude him again. Kathy held her other hand. "Mommy, come on. I want to show you the lanyard I made in crafts."

She was surrounded by competing claimants. The child won, and Alan, looking hurt, went off in search of Sandy. She promised to meet him at the basketball court in time for the evening performance.

Lanyard. A word from the past — not heard since her Girl Scout days, when hers had had to be rebraided three times. Kathy's was neat and trim, like Kathy herself. Where had this sure-fingered, sure-footed child come from?

"Nice work," said Sarah's mother. "Now it's time for everyone to start back toward the lake." In the friendliest possible way, but with a tone used to taking command, she shepherded them out the door and down the grassy bank. Was this how she had spoken to the expedition in Kenya?

The camp PA system bellowed continuous appeals. "Please leave the dining hall and the cabins. The evening program is about to begin. Parents are to be given first priority in seating. No smoking, parents. No shoving, campers."

Adults and children emerged from camp buildings that looked like a fake pioneer village, as if a giant had been playing with a Lincoln Log set. They moved obediently across a field used during the day for basketball, the hoop still visible in the fast-fading light, to where large numbers of folding chairs had been set out in rows. Behind a makeshift curtain small forms seemed to be moving continuously, sometimes piling up in corners with loud thumps and yelps of protest. "I've got to go now," Kathy announced. "I'm make-up."

"What about Jeff?"

"Didn't he tell you? He's the lion."

Childless, she began to look for Alan. She saw him frantically waving from the other side of the basketball court. He had succeeded in saving two seats from the onslaught of several large, healthy-looking campers.

"For God's sake, let's sit down," he said. Most of the folding chairs were already occupied. The moment the sun went down she began to shiver. If only she had remembered how cold the nights were in the mountains, even in July. She should have brought her old fisherman's sweater. Alan put his arm across her shoulders. His fingers were warm against her bare skin. This was the first time he had touched her. She looked quickly around to see if any other parents, or even children, had noticed.

He laughed. "Don't worry, Laura. You haven't been compromised. At least not yet."

Her face reddened. He seemed uncannily aware of what she was thinking. He took off his jacket and draped it carefully around her shoulders. She noticed he was wearing a flannel shirt. Odd that he was so well prepared, and she so disorganized. Perhaps this was the weekend, as well as the summer, for changing roles.

The frenzy of movement behind the curtain now reached a pitch that threatened to dislodge it entirely. Then a series of frantic shhhing sounds, like the air being let out of a large tire. At last the curtain rose (or rather was rolled back by two campers) to reveal another world, the world of the jungle. Some of the real trees and bushes had been used as part of the set; others were clearly made of cardboard and papier-mâché. Real and unreal blended together as quiet descended on the audience.

A flute was heard far offstage, then approaching nearer and nearer, the tone sweet and clear in the sharp Vermont air. Laura was completely enthralled. Soon animals began to gather in the clearing, to sing and to dance, and at last to speak, each one explaining his role in the jungle. After a while they began to quarrel. She couldn't follow the argument exactly. They seemed to be making it up as they went along, but there was clearly much anger and disagreement. The bears shook their furry fists in rage and brushed aside a small rabbit, who tried to make peace. The snakes hissed alarmingly, and the squirrels chattered in fear.

Suddenly a great roar was heard offstage, and the king of the beasts entered, shaking his leonine head. She was glad Kathy had told her. She would never have recognized her son as he presided with grace and dignity over the assemblage. She felt proud as all the other animals bowed down to him.

The various animals presented their versions of the controversy, but she was not really listening. She was too busy watching Jeff insist that each animal be given a fair hearing. At last the matter was settled (all jobs were important, all animals were equally valuable), and harmony restored. The dance resumed, this time with the lion in the center, and the flute was joined by drums, triangles, and cymbals. She turned to Alan in amazement. "He's never anything like that at home." She realized that in her excitement she had taken Alan's hand and clasped it tightly.

He laughed, this time not letting go of her hand. "Neither are you, I'll bet."

SHE DECIDED TO IGNORE THIS REMARK and its implications. Right now she needed to find Jeff. She pulled her hand loose (today she seemed to be constantly connecting and disconnecting — it made her realize again how essentially solitary her life in the past few weeks had become) and pushed through the mob of proud parents and sweaty performers. She found Jeff with his ordinary head, but the rest of him still clothed in bright yellow terry cloth and a long wiry tail. She clasped one of his paws. "Honey, you were terrific. Dad would have been proud of you."

As she spoke she realized how much she was missing Tom. This was a time when the two of them should have been together. There was no one else who shared her exact degree of pride in seeing their shy daughter turn public cartwheels, or their impulsive son perform with such royal dignity.

It was not much fun being a single parent on parents' weekend. Out of the corner of her eye she saw Enid hugging Sarah, her face soft with a similar solo pride. Sarah had been the flute player. Did she have a father, or didn't he care?

The loudspeaker was now instructing all parents to leave the camp immediately. After breakfast they would be welcome for another round of exhibitions, swimming this time. The director seemed to feel that it would be dangerous to leave parents and children alone together for more than a few minutes without a planned activity. Perhaps he was right. She sensed a certain relief as they said good night and parted, the children linking arms and singing as they tramped back to their parentless cabins, the adults hobbling slowly up the stony path to the parking lot. Some were in couples, but like Laura and Enid, many were alone. Enid asked if she had a car. Laura offered Alan's. They were all going to the same hotel, taken over by the camp for the weekend.

He was waiting by the gate of the parking lot, flashing his flashlight at each body that stumbled forward, and looking worried. He smiled with relief when he saw her emerging from the pine trees. "I thought I had lost you. Sandy wanted me to meet his counselor."

She introduced Enid and the three of them squeezed into the front seat of the car. Instant intimacy. Enid's thigh, although close, seemed cool and ladylike. Alan's seemed warm, almost quivering. She wondered if he had a fever. She stifled the impulse to feel his forehead.

The hotel was large and Victorian, its eaves edged with scrollwork. A long string of old-fashioned rockers and white wicker chairs was lined up on the porch.

"Would you like a drink?" Alan addressed both of the women, but he was clearly looking at Laura. Enid said no thank you. She had had a long day, the bus ride had been incredible, and what she wanted more than anything else was sleep.

Alan and Laura sat in matching rockers, sipping Dubonnet, breathing in the clear piney air. Fireflies appeared and disappeared, like small messengers from other planets. A large dog who seemed to belong to the hotel sniffed them, then moved on to explore other guests. Her head felt empty, relaxed, her limbs pleasantly light.

For the first time, she began to think about the man sitting beside her as a possible lover. It was dark on the porch, but she could tell that Alan was as aware of her as she was of him. She was monogamous by temperament and by habit. But strange thoughts had been awakened by her visit to the playground. She had begun to allow herself to feel some of the pain and anger (there was a lot of anger) left over from the summer three years before.

Tom had done it. Why shouldn't she? Laura hadn't found the idea particularly appealing in the abstract — she was too comfortable with the role of victim to think in terms of revenge. But since she had been alone in the city, she had begun to feel differently about herself. No longer an indissoluble part of a legal twosome, an undynamic duo, she was now a woman capable of acting on her own.

It was ridiculous for a woman of her age to have made love with only one man. Besides, Alan was very attractive. There was something about his sensitivity, his awareness of her, even his irresponsibility that excited her. This last surprised her — in the past she had been attracted to responsibleness.

Usually so talkative, Alan was now silent. He seemed restless, no longer content to sit beside her sipping his drink, but getting up frequently to pace up and down the porch. Looking for shooting stars, he told her. There were supposed to be a lot of them in August.

His restlessness was catching. The calm drained out of her, was replaced by prickles of unease. She wondered what she would do if he came to her room or asked her to come to his. She decided not to think about it. For once in her life she was *not* going to plan ahead. After all, this wasn't the kind of item you wrote on a list — have sex with man not husband. She allowed her drink to be refilled by a sleepy boy who seemed too young to be up at this hour, much less serving drinks. They were the only guests still downstairs in the hotel. She felt passive, like a young girl at a dance, waiting to be asked. At last he said, "It's late. Let's go to bed."

They walked up the wide stairway together, holding on to the bannister. Their rooms were next to each other, at the head of the corridor. Alan stood in front of her door as if hesitating. Then he kissed her softly on the lips, turned the key, opened and closed her door. It took her a moment to realize that she was alone in her room, and that he was outside. In a few seconds she could hear him opening his suitcase, running the water in the bathroom next door.

She was surprised at how disappointed she was, like a child whose promised treat is withdrawn at the last minute. How ridiculous. She was at least five years older than he, maybe more. And he would never have believed how inexperienced she was, at least with anybody but Tom. It was better this way. Rationalization nonstop, but not quite fast enough. She felt rejected, led on. She knew that she hadn't imagined the vibrations between them, humming almost from the moment they had met. What had made him change his mind?

She took her toothbrush and soap out of her suitcase and went into the bathroom. She lowered the long flannel granny gown over her head (at least she had remembered — no heat at night in country hotels), and climbed quickly into the high double bed.

She was startled by the sound of a male voice from the armchair. "I don't know whether you look more like Grandma or Little Red Riding Hood."

"Alan, you frightened me. How did you get in?"

He looked pleased with himself. "I just left the door open a little when I said good night."

He shivered. "Christ, it's freezing in here. Mind if I warm up a bit?"

Without waiting for an answer, he slipped under the covers with her. His approach was so obvious, and so unexpected, that she did not have time to protest. Probably she should have been furious, but she wasn't. It was, after all, what she had been waiting for.

They held each other quietly under the heavy quilt for a

long time, and she was beginning to think that perhaps they would just fall asleep like that, two babes in each other's arms, when his hand began to make explorations. She felt her senses beginning to rouse from their long midsummer nap. Her mind was fast asleep, but her nerve endings seemed to be awake and very much in favor of Alan's exploring fingers. Just before the point of no return, her mind woke up and took charge.

She sat up abruptly. "No. That's not what I want." Was it fear of the unknown body, or prudence? It was impossible to tell. "I'm sorry, Alan. I thought that I could, but I can't." She felt as if she might be going to cry. Her first attempt at adultery a failure. "This is new for me."

To her surprise he wasn't angry. "I guess I'm a little out of practice myself." He put his arm around her consolingly, apologetically, as if she were the one who had been disappointed. "It's O.K., Laura. Believe me, it's O.K. Let's just hold each other. That's the best part anyway."

They slid down under the covers again, and this time she was able to relax. After a while, just as she was drifting off to sleep, Alan said, "Would you like to hear my novel?"

She tried to concentrate, but she was very tired. It had indeed been a long day. "Your novel?"

"Yes. I have the manuscript in my suitcase. Wait a minute, I'll get it." He bounced out of bed, full of energy and eagerness once more. In a few minutes he was back, wearing a bathrobe and carrying a box full of at least a ream of yellow paper.

He flipped on the overhead light and seated himself in the armchair. "Now I want you to tell me what you *really* think. You're an editor and I value your opinion."

She tried to shift from woman on the verge of infidelity to evaluator of manuscript by an unpublished author. It wasn't easy. What she really wanted was to close her eyes and go to sleep. They were due back at the camp at ten.

But it was impossible to refuse him. After all, she owed Alan something for her rejection at the last minute. Also, in the back of her brain was an editorial voice that said, "You never know, maybe he *can* write."

His style was strongly influenced by bits of all the writers he had read in college literature courses, but she was trained to sift through the influences to pan for the personal nuggets. Even in the middle of the night, in a cold hotel room in Vermont, she could do it. And there were nuggets. In the midst of long excerpts from "Great Writers I Have Read and Admired" were paragraphs that sounded like Alan. He wasn't afraid to expose himself, to write about real feelings. He might be shy in bed (it was beginning to dawn on her that it hadn't been just her problem) but he seemed a lot less tentative when exposing himself on paper.

"Wait a minute, Alan," she said at last. "Slow down. I can't take it all in, listening. I need to see what it looks like on the page." She climbed down from the bed and took several pencils out of her bag. "Do you mind if I mark it up a little?"

"What's the matter with it? Don't you like it?"

"I *do* like it," she assured him. "But I think that with a few changes it could be even better."

Alan was dubious. "I rewrote it twice," he said. "This is my final copy."

"Of course," she murmured. "I wasn't talking about major changes. Just a little pruning here and there." She was beginning to sound like a gardener.

"All right," Alan reluctantly agreed. "If you think it really needs it."

She slipped into her bathrobe. They moved their chairs together in front of the oak desk and took turns reading pages aloud to each other. "Look," she said, "if you just cut this out, and this, and moved this down here, how much better it would go."

Alan began to be interested. "Maybe we could do the same thing with the next chapter."

They tried various approaches, always checking with the

other to see if they were acceptable. Laura was the one basically in charge, since she was the editor, but Alan, under the
stimulus of her advice, now seemed willing to try almost anything. Some of the best new ideas were his. They were so busy
emending, rearranging, experimenting, that when they looked
up at last, it was almost dawn.

Exhausted but satisfied, they climbed back into the bed and
huddled under the quilt until their combined body warmth
generated enough heat for them to fall asleep.

When Laura awoke a few hours later, she was surprised to
find that she was cradling a man's head against her breast.
Alan sleeping looked even younger than Alan awake. The
balloon at the crafts fair had been misleading. He was not a
giver, but a taker. He was as needy as either of her children.
If she had wanted a third child, though, she would have had
one. She was, she felt, a maternal woman, but not an insatia-
bly maternal woman.

Still, he was appealing. And he did seem to care so much
about what she thought. She would have to look at the manuscript again in the clear light of noon. She had no idea if it
really had the possibilities she had seen in the middle of the
night. Alan's mouth moved against her breast, like a rooting
infant looking for a nipple.

A sudden thought: Had the whole seduction scene been a
ploy to get her to read his novel? Obviously they were both
more comfortable rewriting than making love. She put the
thought out of her mind, slid gently over to her side of the
bed and fell asleep once more.

∞ 8 ∞

SATURDAY IN GENEVA. There was only one way to get through the week, and that was to become a tourist. To pretend that he was in the city for pleasure, and to read the guidebooks looking for pleasurable ways to pass the time.

In New York, when he didn't know what to do with himself, when he needed to get out of the house, he went to the movies. But he had already seen all the American and English movies in the city. Disquieting to hear them dubbed in French, to hear John Wayne or, even worse, Dustin Hoffman, speaking in a cultured Parisian accent. And he had never felt comfortable with French films anyway. He usually let Laura go to them by herself, while he watched the football game on TV.

Geneva, according to the books, was filled with interesting things to do. The aerial tramway to Salève, followed by a brisk hike to the top. Sailing on the lake. Swimming at the beach near the yacht harbor. There was even a heated indoor pool at the Quai de Vernets.

It all sounded too energetic. Good things to do with the kids, or even with Laura, if she was in the mood, but not much fun alone.

He sat in a café, sipping coffee and reading the guidebook's description of the Swiss character. Thorough, clean, orderly, cautious. Hardworking, family loving. All words that could be applied to him as well as to the Swiss. Misleading. Words that hardly described how he was feeling right now. He ought to be making up a list of worthwhile places to see, the United Nations Building, the Reformation Monument, the History of Science Museum which someone had told him had a fine collection of scientific instruments. Instead he sat at a café, watching the Swiss girls go by.

The immediate problem was his laundry. He had a suitcase full of dirty shirts and no idea what to do about them. The hotel had stopped providing laundry service the day the conference ended. The laundresses were probably exhausted by the constant stream of shirts, jockey shorts, and socks, soiled by several groups of international scientists and professors. Doubtless they had all escaped to the Alps to recuperate. The laundresses *and* the professors.

He would like to escape, too. Except that he didn't know exactly when Mr. Torval would arrive, and it was important to be in Geneva when he did. He had been put on permanent hold by the company. By Laura. Damn Laura. She would know what to do about the shirts. Why should he have to sit here on his vacation worrying about laundry?

That sounded terrible. As if her primary function was to keep him supplied with clean clothes. He needed Laura for so much more. To talk to at the end of a long day. To let him burrow between her breasts on a freezing night. To tell him that his tie didn't match his shirt. Shirts again. He must try to stop thinking about them.

Funny that he should miss *that*. It had always infuriated him when she criticized his choice of ties, as if she were the only member of the family with taste, as if her degree in English literature gave her a monopoly on aesthetic sensibility. Goddamn it, chemists had eyes too, even if they hadn't read Blake when they were fourteen. He could tell what went with what as well as she could.

That was just the point. He needed her to argue with, to bounce his ideas against. He hadn't married her just to have a carbon copy of himself. He had valued their differences. The fact that they approached life from different directions, the scientist versus the humanist, made life more interesting. And he had thought she felt the same way. But did she? Did she still find him sexy, funny, smart?

Did anybody, for that matter? It was almost as if, finding himself among strangers for the last month, he had lost his sense of who he was. He had always needed the response of others for reassurance. In high school and college he had hung the awards he won, the diplomas he earned, on the walls of his room, although he knew you weren't supposed to do that. You were supposed to hide them in the bottom drawer of the bureau, as if you didn't care.

Awards for sports were allowed out, cups and trophies, but not certificates of merit for achievement in chemistry, for best exhibit at the science fair, most promising experiment in the university lab. These were supposed to be kept in the closet.

They were there now, at the top of his clothes closet in the apartment, along with the canceled checks for the past ten years and his notes from graduate school. It was hard to believe that in high school he had been voted "Most Likely to Succeed." Whatever his classmates had had in mind (and they had only been responding, after all, to *his* sense of the future) hadn't happened.

If his father had not been carried off by viral pneumonia, while his mother and he stood helplessly by, watching him struggle to bring air into his choked-up lungs, would he now be disappointed in his son? He had always said, "Tom is the one I'm counting on. He's going to make a real contribution."

But he hadn't. He had done some good work, some useful work. But nothing substantive. Nothing that would prompt the King of Sweden to call. Or his father to beam down from heaven.

Enough fantasy. His character hadn't changed totally. He

would emulate the Swiss and make a plan. Today he would buy presents, useful presents that would show both thoughtfulness and taste. Laura was the present buyer in the family, but he could find gifts they would like, that would make them glad to see him when he came home.

He found his way to the Old City, where the guidebook said the best shops were. The Rue du Marché was jammed with tourists, cameras over one shoulder, string bags filled with purchases over the other. He worked his way through the crowds to the shops.

First a Swiss Army knife for Jeff. He should love that. It had ten attachments, including a staple remover and a corkscrew. Next a music box for Kathy. A little store on a side street was filled entirely with music boxes in the shapes of Alpine cottages, grand pianos, castles, carousels. It was almost impossible to choose. He finally bought a small white box with a dancer in a pink tutu on top. When opened, it played "Raindrops Falling on My Head." It was only when he was outside, feeling pleased with himself, that he remembered Jeff was the one who liked music and Kathy was the one who was good with her hands. Too late — he couldn't give Jeff the music box with the dancer. And even if he didn't use the knife much, he could show it to his friends.

Laura's present would be the hard one. He decided to put that chore off for now, and look for a watch for himself. Switzerland was obviously the ideal place to buy a watch. The shops were filled with watches and clocks of every make and type, digital, quartz, guaranteed underwater, underground, even in orbit. There was even one run by a miniature computer that told the time in all the major cities of the world. That was the one he really wanted, but it cost two thousand dollars. He would have to wait until it was mass produced, or at least produced a little more. He and the owner of a tiny shop hidden between a bakery and a delicatessen spent almost half an hour discussing its delicate temperament, its superior performance. This was the kind of discussion he really enjoyed.

A whiff of garlic from the delicatessen reminded him that he had forgotten about lunch. He would leave his pursuit of the perfect watch for another day. The investigation was, after all, the interesting part. He already had a watch.

Time out for food, and perhaps some meditation on the proper gift for Laura. First an easier choice — what to have for lunch? He decided to let the man behind the counter choose for him — a hard crusty roll, a chunk of cheese, and several slices of spicy sausage, origin unknown. In Italy or even in New York he would never have left the choice to another, but there was something about the sparkling showcase and the spotless apron of the proprietor that inspired trust. Next door at the bakery he bought two cream-filled cakes and a small bar of orange-flavored chocolate. A far better lunch than he had had in all his conference sessions at the hotel, where the menu was carefully homogenized to offend — and thus interest — no one.

He took his purchases to a small bench near the Rhône where he could watch the fountain spurting tons of sparkling water into the air. It was almost like a picnic. He remembered the last picnic he and Amy had had in Central Park. He had brought the food, since she didn't seem to care what she ate, and they had sat on the steps of the Bethesda Fountain, watching the kids playing guitars and swapping joints.

He had felt young and carefree, like a schoolboy on a holiday; but the next day *his* joints had ached from sitting so long on the cold stone, and after that, they usually lunched in restaurants. Had it really been the stone steps that made him uncomfortable, or was it the flower children, so much closer to Amy's age than to his? With her long straight hair and thong sandals, she looked ready to join them.

Sometimes in her apartment she played folk songs on her guitar for him. They were not the ones that he and Laura knew from their courtship days. She played songs from her student days in Berkeley, songs of anger at the Establishment, the exploiters of the young, the poor, the black.

He had sat, not paying much attention to the words, watching the way her eyes flashed and her shining dark hair fell over her face. She was so intense as she sang about the plight of the grape pickers that she almost seemed to forget he was there, while he wondered if there would be time to get her into bed before he had to go home.

She was usually more relaxed, more receptive, after she had been singing. It was as if some of the intensity that she poured into her life, her work, her friendships, had been diverted, leaving her softer, more open to him. Sex with Amy was erratic. On days when she was feeling restless, self-critical, it was hard to reach her. But, unlike the Laura of recent years, she was always ready to try something new. And when it was good, it was superb.

Not a good idea to spend so much time thinking about Amy, especially when he had decided never to see her again. He got up and began to stroll along the banks of the river, breathing the clear unpolluted air. For a New Yorker the oxygen content was dangerously high. Swans scudded by; the sun sparkled on the snowy upper slopes of Mont-Blanc. He felt as if he were walking through a picture postcard.

The present. He must concentrate on the present. A pun he had not intended. He always had trouble buying presents for women, starting with his mother. She had praised him for his choices, the handkerchiefs with her initials, the perfume, the scarves, but he always had the feeling that she had not really liked what he had bought for her.

In the beginning he had been able to buy presents for Laura. Their first Christmas together he had bought her the collected works of Jane Austen and she had been pleased. She had read *Pride and Prejudice* to him while he had painted the walls of their tiny apartment. She had loved the string of baroque pearls he had found in a store in the Village for her twenty-fifth birthday. But lately he seemed to have lost the knack of guessing what she would like. She always thanked him, but he noticed she didn't always read the books and that she didn't wear the jewelry very often, except when they went out by themselves. Last year he had suggested that perhaps she would prefer a check. When he said this, her eyes had filled with tears, so he continued in his dogged pursuit of the perfect present.

The children had no such problem. They had merely to paste a few snips of colored paper on oak tag, scribble their names and write "I love you Mommy," and Laura was delighted.

As Suzanne had been with the scarf he bought her from the peddler. And Amy had been with the little gifts he had brought her — leather belts, jars of honey, enamel earrings. Perhaps it wasn't women he had trouble buying presents for. Only Laura.

By now he had strolled away from the river and the swans. Mont-Blanc was hidden behind a cloud. He had reached the Reformation Monument, which one guidebook writer had described as "the most stern and dour creation of the sculptor's chisel that I have ever beheld."

He saw what the writer meant. A long wall of heavy stone interspersed with the forbidding figures of the leaders of the Reformation. Calvin, Farel, Beze, Knox, all stared down at him disapprovingly, their mouths stern and uncompromising behind their long stone beards.

And he knew why. He was a man who couldn't figure out what his wife might want for a present. He had gotten out of the habit of thinking about Laura, except as someone who was always there.

He had a good excuse, one that he was sure would be acceptable to the stone figures looking down on him so severely. He had been preoccupied with his work, absorbed in his own worries about himself, his feeling that he had not done with his life all that he meant to do. They would approve of that.

In the meantime, back in New York, Laura might be slipping away from him. Tonight when she called, he would try to talk to her. It was surely not too late.

∼∼ 9 ∼∼

OF COURSE THE THOUGHT CAME BACK. She hadn't been a trained brooder for twenty-five years for nothing. One got in the habit, like biting one's nails, or eating Mallomars secretly.

They were speeding toward the camp, already late for the swimming exhibition (Sandy was to be in this one), unbreakfasted and underslept. They had hardly spoken this morning, jumping out of the bed they had shared and into their clothes, like two wind-up toys programmed only for parenthood.

She sneaked a glance at Alan, who for once kept his eyes on the road. "Sandy will never forgive me if I'm late." She retreated to her suspicions. A new and more disturbing one appeared. Had Alan *and* Caroline planned the script together? He wanted to be published; Caroline, as his therapist, wanted him sexually active. Laura remembered now Caroline's comments at the craft fair about how Laura would be "good" for Alan. No, that was too paranoid even for her.

Another disquieting memory. The knowing smiles of the couple from the next room as the four of them had emerged simultaneously, almost bumping into each other in their haste to get downstairs and into their cars. Weren't they the parents of a boy in Jeff's bunk? What would they think of her? She felt like whipping out a memo pad from her bag and making herself a small sign to carry. "We didn't do it."

She pictured the knowing smiles slowly changing to contempt and disbelief. "You didn't? Why the hell not?"

This was ridiculous. She couldn't flagellate herself for both what she had and hadn't done. The powerful engine of the BMW brought them to the gate of the camp at the moment that she decided to stop thinking, at least until she had had her coffee.

Alan came to a quick stop in the parking lot. Was it just yesterday that she had been pulled from this car and down this rocky path by Jeff? Alan leaped out of the car and started toward the waterfront, suddenly remembered her, and ran back. He kissed her then, and it was not a tentative kiss. "I like you," he said, and his smile eased her doubts. A minute later, stumbling down the path to the lake, she thought, We both got what we wanted, whatever that was.

The camp director was merciful. He had provided a large urn of coffee and a steaming mound of blueberry muffins for the parents, most of whom were moving slowly, as if still half-asleep. The children, on the other hand, were full of energy, tumbling down the hill like puppies in their eagerness to show their parents how they could swim, dive, and lifesave.

She could see Sandy jumping up and down on the dock. His group was supposed to take a canoe to the middle of the lake, tip it over, and turn it right side up without losing canoe or campers. She held her breath until each of the five bobbing heads reappeared. Sandy's wet red hair gleamed triumphantly in the morning sunlight as he paddled back toward the shore.

This time it was Alan's turn to feel proud. "He could barely swim at the beginning of the summer," he told her. "This is an amazing place."

Now only a few minutes remained before the parents would be asked to leave. Time for the adults and children to recom-

mence their separate summer lives. The children drifted between their parents and the young college students who were
their counselors, not sure where their allegiance lay. But the
summer and the schedule favored the counselors, and the children were moving toward them, calling to each other about
their plans for the afternoon. One little girl dashed up to another asking, "Are yours gone yet?"

Better to leave gracefully now, before they were forced out,
pursued with whips, cattle prods, lists of next week's activities. She looked around for Alan and for Enid, who would be
joining them on the ride back to New York.

But wait a minute. Someone from the other side was approaching. It was Jeff, his face worried, almost adult. "Mom,
I need to talk to you. Alone."

She walked with him to an empty corner of the archery
field, her heart starting to beat a little faster. What was on
his mind? Privacy secured, he seemed speechless. At last he
burst out, "Are you and Dad all right?"

"All right? How do you mean?"

His words came out in a rush. "Well, there's this boy in my
bunk" — here her heart stopped almost completely, then resumed at a gallop — "and his parents are divorced and the
way he found out was when his mother stayed at home for
the summer and his father went to Europe by himself."

Having said his piece, he stared down at his sneakers as if
he might never be able to speak again. How many times, lying
in the dark in his bunk, had he rehearsed it?

Laura took his hand. "Jeff, it's not like that at all. I just
felt that I needed a little time to myself, and Dad had a conference in Geneva." How to explain it to a ten-year-old boy
when she knew she hadn't been able to make his father understand? What was it she had needed time for so urgently, anyway? A chance to snuggle under the covers with Sandy's
father?

But that was her problem. Not Jeff's. Not even Tom's. She

put her arms around her son. "Look, Jeff, Daddy had to stay a little while longer in Geneva to meet a man from Norway." The mythical man from Norway — for the first time she wondered if he really existed. "He wanted me to join him and I would have except that I also wanted to be here with you and Kathy. If I could have split myself in two, I would." Nonsense, that's what she'd been doing all her life. This summer, she suddenly knew, was her attempt to make her life whole, to mend the split.

She kissed him lightly on the forehead. "I'm calling Dad the minute I get home. I'll tell him all about the weekend, and everything you and Kathy did."

To her relief, the cloud lifted from Jeff's face. Whatever she had said, it seemed to have reassured him. The concept of a split mother perhaps — it was what he was most used to. A boy came running up with the news that there would be a free swim before lunch. Jeff bounded after him, like Harold released from his cage. "So long, Mom. Don't worry, I'll write."

The whole camp headed toward the cabins and their bathing suits. As usual, Uncle Manny's strategy worked. She and Enid and Alan left their children splashing happily in the lake. The sound of the swimming counselors' buddy whistles was audible even from the parking lot.

"You look tired, Laura," Enid said solicitously. Laura searched her face for implications that she might need a rest after her strenuous night, but could find none. "Why don't you take a nap in the back for part of the ride?"

Grateful, she sank down among the blankets and old newspapers and dozed for the next few hours. She was awakened finally by hunger and the sound of Enid laughing at something Alan had said. Had she suggested a nap for Laura because she wanted to be alone with him?

Suspicion was malignant. It seemed to grow so swiftly, to corrupt everything in its path, casting a pall on ordinary, kindly actions. Enid, hearing her stir, seemed glad to see her awake. "Up at last. Good. Then we can stop for some lunch and I can talk to you."

No picnic this time, no elaborate staging of sylvan rites, but a straightforward friendly conversation over grilled cheese sandwiches in a roadside diner. Then alternating periods of talk and silence, until the familiar Sunday night crawl across the bridge and down Riverside Drive brought Laura to her apartment a little after nine. Both Alan and Enid shook her hand. Alan told her he would call her soon.

When she opened the door she sniffed. There was a slight but unmistakable odor. Tom and the children often teased her about her supersensitive nose. When she entered a room in which someone had lit a match five minutes before, she usually asked, "What's burning?"

She put down her suitcase and followed the scent from room to room. It was stronger near the bedrooms. In a few minutes she had located its source. Harold lay on his back in his cage, his small, furry legs standing stiff and straight up, his food dish and water bottle empty.

Hesitantly she put one finger through the bars of the cage and touched him. The hamster was very cold. A shudder of revulsion. She had never touched a dead animal before. Tom had always been the one to dispose of pet goldfish, lizards, mice.

Harold's eyes, usually so bright and beady, were clouded over. How could she have forgotten about him, she who had always been a life-enhancer, the family's chief feeder and nurturer? Now she was a murderer. There was no doubt in her mind that that was the right word.

Saturday morning, just before she left, Laura had planned to fill Harold's dish with his favorite seed mix and to refill his water bottle. She had planned to ask her next-door neighbor to feed him on Sunday. But she had been distracted by Alan's late arrival, by her thoughts about what would happen when he appeared, or what she would do if he didn't.

She left Jeff's room and moved to her own, unable to bear the sight of the small accusing corpse. It was almost as if the gods had exacted retribution for her sins — whether of commission or intent didn't seem to matter.

What was she going to tell Jeff? She could see his face now, mouth open, eyes brimming with tears. "You mean that Harold died because you forgot to feed him?"

She sat down on the bed, suddenly very tired, her own eyes full of tears as she pictured the scene. She would have to think of something to say that would make it sound less terrible. In the meantime, there was the body to dispose of. She couldn't go to sleep with Harold lying dead in his cage.

She was clearly not equipped for a life of independent action and adventure. She needed help, someone to tell her that she was not an exterminator of children's beloved pets.

For a long time Alan's line was busy. In between calls, she paced her room, made herself a cup of tea, went to look at her plants in the dining room. They were flourishing beneath the Gro-Lite; she had remembered to give them a careful watering before she left. At last Alan's voice, sounding annoyed. "I'm sorry, Laura, but what do you expect me to do about it?"

Apparently — hard to believe — none of Sandy's pets had ever died. He suggested that she call Enid. "Animals probably die at the museum all the time."

It was Laura's impression that the animals at the museum were already dead and usually stuffed. She thanked him and hung up. It had helped a little to hear another human voice. It didn't really surprise her that Alan had not been able (or willing) to help.

Feeling foolish, she found Enid's number in the book under E. Sims. Unlike Alan, Enid was not annoyed. Her tone was brisk and reassuring. "How old was the animal?"

Laura tried to remember. Jeff had brought him home from third grade at Christmas time, had fallen in love with him, had persuaded his teacher to let him keep him. Harold must have been at least two and a half years old, maybe more.

"Harold was an elderly hamster," said Enid. "Hamsters rarely live longer than three years, most not as long as that. And they don't starve to death in one day. Harold undoubtedly would have died of old age in a few months anyway."

Just a little bit of animal euthanasia. She only hoped that Jeff could see it that way.

"Thank you, Enid. You have no idea how much better you've made me feel. I was almost ready to turn myself in to the captain of the twenty-fourth precinct." Laura tried to keep her tone light, but her voice quivered.

Enid said, "Why don't we meet for lunch tomorrow? I have a busy day, but I think I can take off for an hour." Without waiting for an answer she told Laura to meet her at one at the Seventy-seventh Street entrance near the museum's gift shop. "Now dispose of Harold and get some sleep."

Without touching his body, she wrapped Harold in a newspaper, then placed the newspaper in a plastic bag. She murmured "Rest in peace" as she deposited the package in the garbage can at the back door of her apartment. By the time she awoke tomorrow, she hoped he would be gone.

She undressed quickly and slid under the cool covers of her own bed. How good it was to be home again after her voyage of semi-discovery. Just before she fell asleep, Laura realized that she had forgotten to call Tom in Geneva.

New York was in the grip of a virulent August heat wave. A cloud of heavy damp air hung over the city, blotting out the sun. Every afternoon thunder rumbled in the distance, but no rains came. That week Laura stayed in her air-conditioned bedroom, venturing out only for essential errands — a daily visit to the fruit and vegetable stand, a trip to Wickerson and Lowe to hand in her edited manuscripts and pick up new ones. And her lunches with Enid.

It was a long time since Laura had made a new friend. A long time, too, since a friendship had developed with such swiftness and intensity. It made her think about the summer when she had first met Rachel, the summer they had both been thirteen. Long hot afternoons on the cool side of the house sitting in the grass swapping secrets, telling jokes, planning their lives.

On Monday Laura and Enid lunched in a glassed-in sidewalk café directly across from the museum, the West Side's way of being outdoors and indoors at the same time. They did not mention Harold. Instead they talked about their daughters.

Laura said that she had hoped her first child would be a girl. She had thought that being female, she would understand a girlchild better than a boy. To her surprise Kathy was the mystifying one. She was much more able to guess what Jeff was thinking. In fact, in every way he was the one who was more like her.

Enid agreed that daughters were not always miniatures of their mothers. "Sarah sometimes looks at me with a look that terrifies me. It's so judgmental."

It was hard for Laura to picture Enid being frightened of anyone, but she knew what Enid meant. Kathy's cool gray eyes often seemed to say, "Is this what happens to you when you become a mother?"

Laura asked questions about Enid's job at the museum, her trips to Asia and Africa looking for fossils, her lecture tours. Enid was off on one next week, was frantically trying to get the specimens, the slides, and even the itinerary together. She wanted to hear about Laura's work too, although Laura felt free-lance editing was an unglamorous profession.

"All professions are unglamorous once you're in them," Enid assured her. "Digs are tiring, hot, and dirty. It's months, sometimes years, between real finds. I envy you your immersion in literature, your meetings with writers."

Laura tried to tell her that most manuscripts were badly written, it wasn't the same as reading for one's own pleasure. As a freelance editor she rarely had a chance to meet writers. The ones she did meet seemed to whine a lot or to need almost constant reassurance. It was true that Laura liked working with words, had always liked it. And there was always the chance that she might come across something good.

"In some ways our professions are the same," Enid said. "We're both looking for buried treasure in unlikely places."

Later that afternoon someone in a passing car fired a gun at a man standing in front of the café, shattering the windows and sending the customers under the tables. Laura read about it in her morning *Times,* thinking that if Enid hadn't had to go back to the museum, they might have been sitting there, lingering over iced tea, when the shot was fired.

On Tuesday they decided to lunch in the museum cafeteria. They were constantly interrupted by people coming up to ask Enid's advice on urgent projects. On Wednesday she suggested they meet in her office, where it would be quieter. She turned off the phone and told her secretary to hold all calls. Then she turned to Laura and said, "Tell me about Tom. What kind of man is he?" Until now, their husbands (if indeed Enid had a husband) had gone unmentioned.

A hard question. It was easier for her to describe the young man she had married twelve years before — ardent, ambitious, idealistic, sometimes even a little pompous as he lectured her fiercely on the decaying state of the world. What was Tom like now?

For the last few years Tom's responses had seemed muffled. He had become opaque to her, like a cardboard figure, one of Kathy's paper dolls. It was a long time since he had talked to her about what he was doing in his laboratory. A long time since he had told her his dreams, either waking or sleeping. (When they were first married, they used to lie in bed in the morning, reciting their nighttime adventures, amazed at the creatures they became when they closed their eyes.) Perhaps Tom had stopped having dreams.

The night before, Laura had finally made her call to Geneva. She described Kathy and Jeff's performances in detail as she had promised. "How did you get to the camp?" Tom had asked. (So many of their conversations had to do with logistics.) "Another parent," she had answered. He had found a present for her. "Something I know you'll like. Or rather, I hope you'll like." She hoped he would too. Life would be much easier if she could like the presents he bought for her. Lately, they seemed like the kind a secretary would buy for the boss's wife, except that Tom didn't have a secretary.

Enid listened quietly, then asked, "Any affairs?"

Laura blushed. "Me or him?"

Enid laughed. "Either. You don't have to answer if you don't want to. Forgive me, I'm just interested in other people and how they manage their lives."

Until today, Laura had never spoken to anyone about her fears about Tom's fidelity. Almost as if talking about it would make her suspicions solid, more real. She had not needed sympathy, she had just needed to believe that what she was fairly sure was happening, was not happening. And whatever it was, it seemed to have stopped. Tom and she were not as close as they had once been, but at least it was not like that awful summer, when there had seemed to be no connection between them at all.

"And you? How did it go with Alan?"

"It didn't. At least not in the way it usually does." Enid roared with laughter as Laura told her about the all-night session with Alan and his manuscript. "A night to remember." Laura wondered if Enid was making fun of her, but her laughter seemed good natured, rather than mocking. "It's your turn. What about your husband, Enid?"

"Oh Edward." She dismissed him with a wave of her hand. "He's not my husband anymore. Probably never should have been either, poor man. But he served his function. He gave me Sarah. And he takes good care of her while I'm away."

Laura felt the first chill in their new friendship. Presumably Edward was a person with feelings, desires, needs. He was also Sarah's father.

Enid leaned forward and took her hand. "I see you don't like my attitude toward Edward. I don't like it much myself." She stood up abruptly. "Time to get back to work. Shall we meet tomorrow? I want you to suggest some books for me to read in hotel rooms in Ohio, North Dakota, and Wyoming. Lecture tours are the only chance I get to read."

On her way down the long flight of marble stairs from Enid's office Laura thought, We never talked about her affairs, only mine. She lingered in the dark cool hall of the African mammals, reluctant to re-enter the simmering New York outside. She had not been in this hall for many years. She stared at the giant eland with its beautiful twisted horns, the okapi, and the gembok, animals she had grown accustomed to thinking of as existing only in crossword puzzles. She remembered Kathy as a curly-headed three-year-old in the huge hall of the dinosaurs, clutching her hand and murmuring over and over, "They used to be alive, but they're not alive now. They used to be alive, but they're not alive now."

She wandered through an exhibit of photographs, "The Unseen Flowers of the Desert." Tiny beautiful plants, magnified many times. She stepped away from the photographs and craned her neck upward to read the caption on the wall. "Like other desert plants, these miniatures may bloom only once in many years, when the temperature and moisture are just right. Then they race through growing cycles, explode, and bloom, sometimes only for a few hours, and are gone in a flash until next time."

Like me this summer, she thought, blooming in the desert of New York. For the first time in many years, life was full of possibilities. She only hoped that they would not prove to be as ephemeral as the flowers.

She stepped out of the museum and into the blinding sunshine of Central Park West. It was too hot for the subway. She waited for a bus, hoping it would be air conditioned. It wasn't. In the seat behind the driver sat a man wearing a

heavy coat, a wool scarf, and earmuffs. Unlike the other passengers, he seemed unbothered by the heat. In the climate of
his mind it was midwinter. Laura was so absorbed in watching
him (he didn't seem to mind, or even to notice) that for quite
a while she didn't see Alan waving to her from the back of
the bus.

He was on his way to deliver some layouts to a client in
the Majestic. "Get off the bus with me," he said. "We'll go
some place cool and have a drink."

The place he chose was almost deserted on a weekday
afternoon, an air-conditioned cave filled with Muzak and
stale peanuts. A bargirl swabbed tables dreamily. The bartender poured a green fizzing liquid into an amber glass,
watching himself and them in the shadowy mirror.

Alan, however, was not in a dreamy mood. He was full
of new ideas, new plans. He was going to quit the advertising
business, get a part-time job as a waiter, or maybe even a
bartender. "That way I'll have more time to write. You've
changed my whole life, Laura. I hope you realize that."

She looked at him in alarm. "I was a dilettante before,"
he went on. "Now, thanks to your encouragement, I've become a serious writer."

"What about Sandy? Children are so expensive," she murmured.

"We'll manage. We always have. I'm going to tell them at
the end of the week." He grabbed her hand. "Have dinner with
me to celebrate on Saturday?"

Enid was coming to dinner on Saturday, a farewell evening
before her trip. "I'll come too," said Alan. "We'll make it a
joint celebration." He sensed her hesitation. "What's the
matter, Laura? Are two new people in your life too much
for you?"

"Of course not." Enid and Alan already knew each other,
even seemed to like each other. Why was she hesitating?
Perhaps because she wanted to talk to Enid without interrup-

tion about some of the subjects they had touched on in their lunches. (At the museum she was constantly aware of the insistent pull of Enid's work. Today, even as they talked in her office, she had watched the lights flashing imperiously on the phone, callers whose rings were no less urgent because silent.) Subjects that would be of no interest to Alan — or even to Tom.

Laura noticed that Alan had not asked her how she was, or what had happened to her since her frantic Sunday phone call. He only wanted to tell her how she had changed *his* life.

As if to refute her silent condemnation, he said, "Laura, you haven't heard a word I've said. What's been happening to you this week? I really would like to know." Would he? She decided to give him the benefit of the doubt. "Yes, come on Saturday, Alan. We'll have a real party."

"Only if you'll let me cook. I'm a first-class wok wielder. I'll be in Chinatown on Friday afternoon, so I'll buy all the stuff then and drop it off at your place Friday evening."

This time he didn't ask, he just told her. She was intrigued by the idea of Alan's preparing a meal for them. That would leave her free to try out her new role as woman enjoying simultaneous complex relationships.

Alan squeezed her hand. "Good. Then it's settled. And after Enid goes home we can really talk." His smile was so broad it could only be called a leer. The evening might become more complex than she had planned.

∞ *11* ∞

CAROLINE CALLED ON THURSDAY MORNING, enraged. "What are you doing to Alan? I've never seen him in such a state. He doesn't know whether he's coming or going."

"I haven't done anything to him. Nor has he done anything to me."

"I know. That's what I'm calling about. He finally gets up the nerve to make the big approach and then you turn him down. Do you realize what that means? It may be months, even years, before he tries again."

Now she was enraged. "Caroline," she shouted into the phone, to both Caroline's and her own surprise. "What are you, a therapeutic pimp? Whatever Alan and I do, or don't do, is our own business." She slammed down the receiver so hard that it seemed to bounce. She had always considered herself a private person. Now the events of her life seemed to be public property. Caroline was probably calling Lydia right now. "Have you talked to Laura lately? She's acting very strangely. All I said was . . . "

She didn't care what Caroline said. She had thoroughly enjoyed slamming down the receiver. Physical violence, even of a minor kind, had until now been foreign to her. Once, a

long time ago, when she had had a long frustrating rainy day
with the children and Tom had walked in asking when supper
would be ready, she had picked up his umbrella, dripping in
a corner of the front hall, and thrown it at him. He had
ducked and the umbrella had hit the radiator. She still
remembered the children and Tom staring at her with
their mouths open, as if she had suddenly turned into a fire-
breathing dragon. It had been a moment of heady power, never
repeated.

The next phone call was from Enid. She couldn't meet
Laura for lunch. A new shipment of material had just come
in from Nairobi, and it would take her all day and most of
Friday to unpack and label it. She sounded genuinely sad,
as if she would have preferred to be with Laura. Also eager
to get off the phone and find out what was in those boxes.
"I have an idea. I'm going to my health club tomorrow night
for a swim. Why don't you join me there?"

The third call was from Lydia. She had indeed been talking
to Caroline (she didn't say so — Lydia, unlike Caroline, was
always discreet — but Laura could tell). The Fourth of July
painting had become a series of paintings. She was working
on panel number two of a triptych of Catherine wheels. The
evening in Riverside Park had altered her entire approach to
painting. She proposed lunch.

Laura said not today, maybe next week. She sensed a tone
in Lydia's voice that said, "Changes are taking place in my
life, changes that have nothing to do with painting, that I
need to talk about."

Next week Laura would listen, sympathize, commiserate,
whatever was needed, but now she preferred to be alone. It
was time to look at the manuscripts sitting on her desk in
the bedroom. She had two to edit by September first. One
was a lightly disguised account of the male author's recent
divorce from a well-known actress. The other, a middle-aged
woman's first-person account of the six weeks she spent in a

Nebraska commune. Laura wondered if the ex-husband and the ex-commune member would like each other. Probably not. They were both too busy exploring their own sensations to notice anybody else.

She had already spoken to Mr. Lowe about Alan's novel. "Send me fifty pages and I'll take a look," he had said, sending Alan into a frenzy of hope, although Laura had told him that this was mere courtesy.

"But *you* liked it," said Alan, his arms full of Chinese vegetables on Friday night. "Maybe he will too." He instructed her not to open the bags, but to leave them on the kitchen table. "It ruins vegetables to refrigerate them," he told her. "It keeps them from breathing properly." She couldn't tell whether or not he was serious. People today seemed to feel intensely about so many things she had never given a moment's thought.

Like Enid and exercise. Apparently she cared passionately about physical fitness. She jogged around Central Park at six-fifteen every morning and swam at her club as many nights as she could manage. The very thought made Laura recoil — her idea of bliss was sitting in front of a roaring fire or under a beach umbrella with a good book.

"You have to keep in condition in my profession," Enid said, and plunged into the waters of the Olympic-size pool for the first of forty energetic laps. Laura watched her from the side of the steaming pool, marveling at the clean sure way her body cut through the water, one stroke following another, in a steady rhythm. Then Laura lowered herself carefully into the shallow end of the pool and made several brief trips sideways, holding on to the tiles at each side before paddling slowly across. The smell of chlorine was overpowering. The voice of a swimming instructor at the far end of the pool echoed in the enormous room. "Keep your elbows in, fingers curved, knees straight."

She did none of these, but luckily he was too far away to

see. She pulled herself out onto the marble steps, feeling their sharp edges through the ancient nylon of her bathing suit, and stared at her underwater toes. Enid emerged from the other end of the pool, unwinded and full of messianic zeal.

"There's nothing like swimming," she said as they stood under adjoining showers. "You ought to try it. It makes you feel completely alive."

Laura was busy washing off the chlorine and looking at bodies. It had been a long time since she had seen a naked body, except her own and Tom's and the children's. The brief glimpse of Alan as they had dressed on Sunday morning seemed hardly to count, surrounded as she was now by such a great profusion of hips and breasts. In her college days women had always showered separately, emerging from their individual stalls with towels from neck to knees.

It was amazing how different each body looked. There were as many shapes as there were women. Her own breasts and hips were unexceptional, neat and well-made (not sloppy and drooping like that huge woman in the corner, thank goodness) but unexciting. Enid's body was a distinct surprise. In her clothes she looked large-boned but trim, well put together. Undressed, she was completely different. Her figure was rich, lithe, almost luxuriant. Her breasts were large and beautiful, still firm and pointing directly ahead, like those of a young girl.

Enid saw Laura looking at her and smiled. All her movements, as she rinsed and lathered herself, were swift and sure, as if she knew exactly what she looked like, and the knowledge gave her pleasure. Then why, Laura wondered, as they re-entered their clothes, does she always wear straight skirts and tailored blouses, clothes that hide her shape, in fact make one forget about it altogether?

Outside they shook hands and parted, Enid to meet the person who was arranging her lecture tour, Laura to await her call from Tom. "Why don't you try jogging home?" Enid asked as they stepped into the airless smog of Fifty-seventh Street.

How the creatures do order one about, Laura thought crossly. "Jog up Broadway." "Sleep with my patient." "Don't move the Chinese vegetables." And last, a faint voice that she could not entirely banish, "Feed my hamster."

Laura had been planning to walk home. Now she decided to disobey Enid and take the bus. It was full of musicians carrying large instruments — guitars, cellos, even a bass fiddle. She finally found a place to stand in front of a kind-looking elderly man. She felt her bare toe pressing against a box pushed underneath his seat.

"Cut that out," the man growled. "You're kicking my autoharp."

She smiled apologetically and began to inch her way back toward the one available seat. She noticed that everyone on the bus was carrying a large package of some kind. Several seemed to contain animals who mewed or barked or whimpered every time the bus came to an abrupt halt. Even she, who usually traveled light, was holding a shopping bag with her bathing suit, her towel, and her hair dryer.

The bus crawled up Broadway. She hoped she would be home in time for Tom's call. She wondered whether she should tell him about Harold.

It turned out to be almost impossible to tell him anything. The connection from Geneva was full of crackling static, and she could hardly hear his voice. She thought he said that Mr. Torval had finally arrived. She told him some friends were coming for dinner. She asked him what he was doing, but was unable to hear his answer. It was like trying to communicate with someone on another planet, or with a foreigner using an outdated phrase book.

Her sleep was troubled by disturbing dreams. Alan fed Harold, now grown to human size, with large helpings of stir-fried vegetables. Harold fell into a swimming pool located where the dining room used to be, and began to squeak frantically. He was rescued by Enid, who bore him in triumph on her back, her breasts floating before her like white pontoons. Then Enid and Laura dried him off with large fuzzy towels, rubbing back and forth across his furry body until his small pink penis rose and stood straight up. Harold leered and began to come toward Laura.

She woke with her heart pounding. The dream was so vivid that she felt compelled to get up and go into Jeff's room to stare at Harold's empty cage. She picked it up and put it outside the back door. Let it follow Harold, wherever he had gone.

The rooms of the apartment were as hot and steaming as the pool at Enid's health club. It made her feel hotter just to look at the tweedy couch, chosen because it wouldn't show the dirt (it did), the heavy linen curtains bought to keep out the frigid wind from the Hudson (they didn't), Tom's beloved Naugahyde chair. As she got up, she felt her nightgown sticking to the back of her knees.

Outside, she sniffed the familiar chemical smell of New York in the early morning hours. A mixture of burning rubber, melting plastic, and for some reason, the odor of freshly brewed coffee. She hurried back to her cool bedroom, trying not to breathe too deeply on the way. She fell immediately into a deep dreamless sleep from which she rose refreshed, ready to face whatever the day might bring.

∞ *12* ∞

A LAN ARRIVED AT SIX-THIRTY, as sober as a surgeon about to scrub for a major operation. He carried two shopping bags full of what he called his tools — a giant wok with a metal collar, a pair of barbecue tongs, a boning knife, and a lethal-looking cleaver.

"In Chinese cooking the dicing, shredding, and cutting are the most important parts. It's essential that all the knives be razor sharp."

"Can I help?" Laura asked. She was not in the mood for a lecture on the art of Chinese cooking. Or for a lecture on anything, for that matter. Alan had not yet begun to cook, was merely chopping and dicing, but already the kitchen steamed with the fervor of his activity.

He waved her away. If she was not to become a Chinese cooking acolyte — and it was clear she was not — he preferred to have the kitchen to himself.

"Just let me know when Enid comes, so I can time the meal." Before he could tell her that timing (along with chopping) was the essence of Chinese cooking, she slipped into the dining room.

She had already set the table for three, in a spurt of

earlier energy, so there was now nothing to do but wait. Her new sundress, which in a fit of daring she had decided to wear braless, was already sticking to her back and chest. The shirred material stretched taut across her breasts made her remember something she had not thought about in years.

Saturday afternoons with Rachel, in Rachel's mother's sewing room, making costumes out of leftover scraps of materials. Laura remembered the two of them holding triangles of transparent net and organdy across their just-beginning-to-bud breasts, looking shyly at each other, giggling about what it would be like if the boys they knew could see them now. Laura was always acutely aware of Rachel's older brother Larry in the next room, so close and yet so oblivious of what they were doing. Saturday afternoons at Rachel's house had a special feeling of secrecy and excitement.

She could hear the sound of Alan ferociously wielding the cleaver in the kitchen. Enid, who was always so prompt, was almost twenty minutes late. She wondered whether she should move the table into the bedroom, where the air-conditioner was.

Tom and Mr. Torval sitting in a crowded café sipping white wine. He had asked Tom to call him Olaf, and perhaps after another demiliter, he would. Their talks had gone well — they had taken to each other almost immediately, even though Mr. Torval — all right, Olaf — was ten years older than he. Tom had always imagined Norwegians to be cold, restrained, self-contained. Olaf had laughed when he presented this picture. "You must be thinking of the *northern* Norwegians. I was born in the south."

Such subtle distinctions were beginning to blur under the influence of the good Chablis and the chance to talk to someone who seemed to be interested, someone who wasn't a waiter, a shopkeeper, a hotel clerk. Or a wife, three thousand miles away.

〜〜〜

Enid came at last, looking distinctly uncrisp. "It's been a terrible day," she said, flopping down on the couch. "I had lunch with Edward to make all the arrangements for Sarah. After we discuss her dancing class and dental appointments, it's depressingly clear we have nothing more to say. Then, in the middle of packing, the power went off in my building. I had to walk down eighteen flights, and I forgot to bring the wine. I'm sorry."

Laura was startled to see Enid so flustered. She urged her to have a cool drink, to forget about packing, about arrangements. If the power was still off when it was time to go home, she could always stay with her.

In a few minutes Enid seemed to recover. She leaned back against the couch, looking around the room, seeing everything. "This is your room, Laura. It looks the way I thought it would. Serene, tasteful, unpretentious." Laura wasn't sure she liked this portrait of herself. It seemed to leave a lot of parts out.

Alan appeared in the doorway, greeted Enid, announced that the chopping was done, and stretched out on the living room floor with his eyes closed. His arms and legs moved slightly — more like twitches than movement — and he began to hum something under his breath. Probably his mantra, Laura thought. Enid put a finger to her lips. The two women were silent. Eventually Alan sat up, opened his eyes, and shook himself like a puppy emerging from a sprinkler. "That's better." He made himself a drink, grinned at them both, and returned to the kitchen.

〜〜〜

Olaf's wife and three children were waiting for him in Zurich. In a few days they were to take a motor trip through

Italy, perhaps even go to Greece. Last year they had explored the Low Countries. "The best trip we've had so far."

Tom was jealous. They sounded so close, so comfortable with each other. The one time his family had traveled together, more than just a drive to a summer cottage, it had been a disaster. Four of them crowded into one motel room to save money, the children bickering, he snarling at his loved ones, father the arch-fiend. And Laura getting quieter and quieter, constantly swallowing aspirins. It had been a relief to get home where at least the children had separate rooms. Yet, at home they often got along reasonably well. Perhaps that was because they were all basically private people. Especially he and Laura.

Tom was startled to hear Olaf confess, as he stared into his wine as if he were asking its forgiveness for what he was about to say, "Maybe my wife and I travel with the children so much because we're afraid to be alone together."

The dinner was a spectacular success, despite the heat and Alan's constant cries of despair from the kitchen. Laura and Enid sat at the table while he brought in bowls filled with delicious delicacies seasoned with ginger, garlic, sesame: bamboo shoots, bean sprouts, tender chicken, shrimp, and beef. He was at last persuaded to sit down and taste the feast he had prepared. He agreed it was good, that despite his histrionics (or perhaps because of them), this was one of his better nights.

Alan had brought fortune cookies to serve with fresh pineapple for dessert. Laura felt a small shiver of apprehension as she opened hers. Perhaps it would be a clue to the next step in her life, a secret message. She unrolled the tightly furled piece of paper. "Do not be fooled by the words of others."

Enid and Alan peered over her shoulder. Alan said, "And

I was hoping she was going to become a little more trusting."

Enid smiled. "I think she's already far too trusting, as it is."

Laura hated being discussed as if she weren't there. She re-rolled her fortune and asked, "What do yours say?"

Enid and Alan both had the same message. It read, "Desire fulfilled is a tree of life." They looked at each other, then at Laura, waiting to see what her reaction would be. Laura said nothing, not knowing what she could possibly say. Alan laughed uneasily.

Enid said coolly, "Life is too short to be spent interpreting oracles. Could we go into the bedroom? The heat seems to be getting to me tonight."

Again Laura was surprised at her discomfort. She had assumed that since Enid spent part of each year in Africa, she would be impervious to heat. "That's dry heat," Enid explained. "It's the damp dirty kind we have in New York that really does me in." Even her voice seemed faint, as she seated herself in a chair directly in front of the air-conditioner.

Alan, on the other hand, who had spent the evening hovering over a hot wok, seemed full of energy. He sat on the edge of the bed, almost bouncing with vitality, looking from one woman to the other with interest. Laura plunged once more into the steam bath of the rest of the apartment in search of more ice for their drinks.

Mr. Torval — it just wouldn't work, Tom couldn't think of him as anything else, despite the intimate things they were revealing to each other — drank the last of the Chablis and ordered another bottle. He was silent at last, having just finished a long Norse saga of love grown tepid, of the transfer of passion to work, to children, to the pursuit of ideas. "But on a cold Norwegian night, you can't really make love to a concept." He smiled ruefully. "I would not, of course, have told you any of this, if you were Norwegian, or if I thought we would be meeting again." He poured new wine for both of them and touched his glass to Tom's. "In fact, the only reason I have told you these things tonight is probably because you are an American."

He saw Tom's puzzled look. "Americans are supposed to be open, outgoing, full of feeling, are they not? I have always imagined them that way at least."

"You must be thinking of *South* Americans. It's not true about the Americans I know. Certainly it's not true of me." Strange to be sitting across a table from another man, talking about feelings (or even lack of them). A new experience — one that would take getting used to. He asked, "But is there no hope? Maybe if you and your wife had a talk . . . "

"There is no hope. We had our talks years ago. And in truth this arrangement suits us. It seems to be what we both want."

Although the night was warm Tom felt a slight chill, as if a glacier from the North was gradually covering their table with its ice and rocks. He could feel the other pulling back, like a turtle who has made the unaccustomed gesture of sticking his neck out. Both of them now uncomfortable with exposure, with revelations.

Mr. Torval sighed. "Enough about me. Tell me about your marriage, about your good wife back in America."

Laura *was* a good wife, a good person. Theirs was the usual story of familiarity breeding detachment. Except that Tom was no longer feeling detached. If only they could return to those first years of passionate interchange. And Torval asked Tom the same question Tom had asked him. "Have you tried to talk to her? Have you told her how you feel?"

"It's funny. I thought everything was fine until I came to Geneva without her." Tom shifted uneasily in his chair. "I've tried, but it's impossible on the telephone. It's too far away. The connection is bad in every sense." He felt profoundly sad, as if there were no hope anywhere in the world for old lovers.

Mr. Torval leaned forward. Astonishingly, he was gripping Tom's hand. "Then write to her. Tell her how you feel in a letter, a letter she can look at when you are not there. I have a strong feeling that for you it's not too late. Promise me you will do it."

The look on the other man's face — intense, pleading, as if it mattered very much to him what happened to Tom and Laura. Was he as reconciled to his own marriage as he had seemed?

Miraculously, the glacier began to recede. Perhaps he and Laura could be close once more. The sun might even come out in the middle of the night. Anything was possible. It was at least two o'clock in the morning by now, and the waiters were beginning to mop up nearby tables with meaningful swipes.

"I'll do it," Tom almost shouted. "I'll write tonight." He resisted the urge to hug the Norwegian. After all, they couldn't shed all their inhibitions at once — that would be too frightening for both of them. "Thank you, my friend. You may have saved my life."

Olaf Torval stood up and leaned forward in a formal, if slightly wobbly, bow. "My pleasure."

∽ *13* ∽

ALAN HAD GONE HOME AT LAST, carrying shopping bags full of cooking utensils and small plastic containers of leftover spices and vegetables. "Are you sure you don't want me to stay?" he asked, standing at the elevator door, too encumbered to push the button. "I'm a superb masseur. I could teach you the five basic yoga positions."

Enid pushed the elevator button for him and said that the dinner had been delicious. Laura told him she would call him in a few days. Then Enid and Laura sat in the bedroom talking about their childhoods.

Enid had been brought up on a farm in Iowa, Laura in a suburb of Boston. "From the moment I was born," Enid said, "I knew I had to get out. There wasn't anybody for miles around that was anything like me."

She leaned back in her chair, took a long sip of wine, and smiled at Laura. "When did you first know?"

"Know what? That I was going to leave?" Laura thought for a moment. "Not until high school. Every Saturday afternoon I used to take the bus downtown to the one drugstore that carried *The New Yorker*. It didn't get there until Saturday." She sighed. "I still don't have a subscription. But now I can buy it on Thursday."

"Nobody in our part of Iowa had ever heard of *The New Yorker*. The *Farmer's Almanac* was the big seller, next to the Bible. I was ten when my cousin Joe showed me the Song of Songs. What a disappointment when I discovered that it wasn't representative."

The air-conditioner whined reassuringly and the night stretched ahead. It had been decided that Enid would stay, rather than walk up eighteen flights to her airless apartment. Laura was only dimly aware of the steady Latin beat of the music coming from the rooming house next door, of the sirens of the ambulances and police cars on Broadway. The rest of the apartment had ceased to exist. In this room there were two young girls growing up, one in the Midwest and one in the Northeast.

"Did you always want to get married?" Enid asked.

"Of course, and then to have two children, a boy and a girl." Laura laughed. "So you see, my life is a dream come true. My best friend Rachel and I would spend hours discussing the names of our children. It never seemed to occur to us that our husbands might have other ideas."

"Mine didn't," Enid said flatly. "I told him I wanted one child, a daughter named Sarah. In that way, he was a most obliging man."

"I remember the day Tom asked me to marry him." She hadn't been sure she loved him, but it had been exciting to be asked. The next afternoon, she had left her roommates in their apartment on Beacon Hill and walked up and down the steep cobblestone streets, thinking about Tom's proposal. She sat by the pond in the Boston Public Garden, watching families paddling by in the swan boats, her mind in a pleasant blur. Once she had thought, exultantly, If I can get Tom to ask me, I can get anybody. But this thought did not linger. Tom had asked, and she knew that she would almost certainly accept him. He had said he loved her. He was kind, funny, and smart; she was strongly attracted to him, and he came from the kind of family that would please her parents. There was no reason *not* to accept him.

Enid's voice cut through the past. "I never thought I would. Marry, that is. I always pictured myself alone." She sighed and took another sip of her wine. "I couldn't imagine allowing myself to get that close to another person." Curled up in the armchair, she looked for a moment vulnerable, uncertain, not the competent self-assured woman of the daytime. Then the look vanished. "After all, I do have Sarah. I got what I really wanted."

"Yes, we both have the daughters we wanted. They're eight now. Soon they'll be eighteen."

Enid laughed explosively. "The poor things. Don't rush them. God, I'm glad I'm not eighteen anymore."

"Why? What were you like then?"

"Loud, bossy, bumptious. Nobody could tell me anything. I was going to win a scholarship to the state university, then a fellowship to Greece. But underneath, scared as hell. Afraid nobody would like me, that they wouldn't be willing to give me my chance." She slid her long legs out from under her, turning once more into a full-size woman. "And of course I did do all those things. And most of them turned out to be as interesting as I thought they would be. I love my work. Except for Sarah, it's the center of my life."

She turned to Laura. "And you? What were you like at eighteen?"

"Very different from you. Shy, insecure, watching others to see how to act. Wanting to do the right thing. But underneath not really so different. I was a dreamer, too." She was beginning to feel embarrassed, but she couldn't stop, now that she was saying aloud thoughts that had been in her head for such a long time. "I always felt I was going to do something special although, unlike you, I had no idea what it would be. My marks were high, but I knew I didn't want to go to graduate school. And later, even though I was good at editing, I never felt really involved." She laughed nervously. "But then I got married and had children and forgot about it."

Enid was sitting next to her now, holding her hand. "But Laura, you didn't forget. It's all still there." Enid put her arm around her shoulder. "You haven't found your private dream yet. It's so private you don't even know what it is yourself. You're like the princess in the tower. Except that there is no wicked witch. All you have to do is open your eyes and climb down."

Laura said, "Do you really think so?"

Enid said, "I know so. And I'm never wrong."

The beat of the music from next door was now so loud it vibrated in the room as if there were no walls between. Laura felt a sudden surge of excitement. She kicked off her sandals and began to dance around the room. This fall, as soon as the children were safely settled in school, she would start on her quest. She felt a burst of gratitude toward Enid, who had shown her the way. She put her arms around her new friend, and together they improvised a joyful dance to life's possibilities.

Enid was surprising light on her feet. They danced quickly at first, then more slowly, slipping into the close cheek-to-cheek dance of their adolescence. They held each other tightly, their bodies moving softly against each other to the steady beat of the salsa.

It was no surprise to Laura when, as they lay on the bed, exhausted from their dancing, Enid began slowly, lovingly, to make love to her. Perhaps it should have seemed strange to her, but it didn't. Enid's body was a mirror image of her own. She had never been taught to be on guard against her desires for a woman. And Enid's caresses were all familiar, the same ones Laura used in making love to Tom.

At first she lay passively, letting Enid's exploring tongue and fingers bring her to climax again and again, until she felt pleasure over all the surfaces of her body. She lay relaxed and at ease after the long dry summer. Then she began to explore Enid's body, and soon discovered the pleasures of giving as well as receiving, of cradling her head between another woman's breasts, between another woman's legs. This was indeed new territory for her. Soon the doing and being-done-to merged. She was no longer conscious of giving and receiving. She was baby, mother, daughter, lover all at once. As was Enid.

At last they stopped, both of them satisfied. Enid raised herself on one elbow and looked at Laura. "You've never done this before, have you? How do you feel?"

Laura thought a moment, then said with surprise, "I feel fine."

"Good," said Enid. "I'm glad. You're a lovely person. Tonight, even I'm a lovely person." She kissed Laura on each eyelid, then lightly on each breast. "Let's sleep now. By tomorrow afternoon I'll be on a plane to Chicago."

∾ 14 ∾

THE MORNING AFTER. How strange to find herself in bed with a woman. Tom was the first and, until Alan, the only person she had ever shared a bed with. Even as a young child in crowded summer cottages, she had insisted on her own sleeping space. Cautiously, she tested her psyche to see how she felt. Still O.K. Enid, awakening, smiled at her, and she smiled back. Then Enid glanced at the bedside clock. "My God, I've got to run. Make me some coffee, Laura, while I shower."

When Enid appeared in the kitchen she was in her daytime disguise, sensible drip-dry suit, sensible sandals. Her mind was clearly on the trip, her packing, whether there would be much traffic on the way to the airport. Every few minutes she glanced at her watch, although she dutifully ate the grapefruit, whole wheat muffins, and honey that Laura placed in front of her. Laura found herself wishing that Enid would leave so that she could think about the night they had shared. There was little connection between the sensual Enid of the night and the no-nonsense woman sitting across the breakfast table.

At the door to the apartment, one hand on the knob, Enid

paused, suddenly shy. "Look, Laura, I've known I was a lesbian since I was fourteen, but last night doesn't mean you're one. Maybe you're one of those lucky people who can enjoy the best of both worlds. Anyway, whichever way you decide, we'll be friends. Thanks for everything." A quick hug and she was gone.

Leaving Laura to put away the honey jar, wash out the coffee pot, and remake the bed while she wondered, was she or wasn't she? Once one began to explore and not to take oneself for granted, there seemed to be more possibilities than she had imagined. She didn't feel as if she were a different person from the one she had been the day before. True, she felt more physically at ease, more relaxed, but then she always did after good lovemaking. Had she perhaps expected a blaze of light, a finger pointing down from the clouds, as in a Cecil B. De Mille movie? She wondered if she would have been so adventurous if she had not known that Enid was leaving the next day.

Anyway, like most questions except what to have for supper, she didn't have to decide today. There was much to do in the apartment. Tom would be back next week, the children the week after that. She made a list of household chores to be accomplished — rug cleaned, new shelf paper in the kitchen, children's closets to be checked for outgrown clothes — then found herself drawn to the pile of manuscripts on her desk. Enid's presence and departure seemed to have released a source of working energy that had lain dormant for much of the summer. Her sexual and editorial urges seemed oddly intertwined these days.

If only the author who had taken the brisk tour of the nation's communes could be persuaded to tell less about what everyone was wearing and eating, and more about what they were thinking and doing; she never got tired of reading about what people ate in novels, but it was not as interesting if the meals had actually been eaten. When she looked up from the manuscript, it was late afternoon. She decided to go walking in Riverside Park.

She marveled at the great variety of people talking, holding hands, taking licks of the same ice cream cone. It was as if a veil had been lifted from her familiar environment. Father, mother, and two children was only one of many possible combinations. Why had she never realized this before? The intriguing combinations in the park had surely been there all along, but she had noticed only the conventional units, the ones her mother and father would have approved of.

Perhaps this wasn't completely true. She had seldom been in the city in August. This was the month when most people she knew migrated to the Berkshires, to Fire Island, to Cape Cod. Leaving, of course, the unconventional ones, the experimenters. She sat on a bench near the Soldier and Sailor's Monument, licking a chocolate chip ice cream cone and watching the multiracial intersexual parade. At dusk she felt a strange hand on her shoulder, an unknown male voice in her ear. "You look lonely, lady. Want company?"

"No, thanks." She spoke politely, picked up the Sunday *Times* Book Review (the screen for her afternoon couple's survey), and walked briskly toward West End Avenue without looking back. She wasn't frightened as she once might have been. The street after all was full of people. She understood the need for companionship at the end of a long solitary Sunday. But she didn't need any company this evening. There were too many people in her head already, from both the past and the present.

As she lay in a cool bath, enjoying the feel of the water against her re-awakened body, she thought about herself and Rachel. The two of them sitting in a darkened movie house after school on Friday afternoons lusting after Gregory Peck, their hands tightly clasped during the love scenes.

At fifteen Laura and Rachel had exchanged friendship

rings, which they swore never to remove. It was Rachel whom Laura missed most when she went away to college, not her parents, nor the few high school seniors and college freshmen who had kissed her tentatively and awkwardly in her parents' living room, or the back row of the local movie theater.

Rachel was still living in Boston, working in a publishing house (they had both been literary adolescents, yearning after the men in the books they read, Heathcliff, Rochester, Howard Roark). Once a year she came to New York to visit, bringing just the right present for each of them. The children adored her, Tom obviously enjoyed her company, but she and Rachel almost never spoke to each other alone.

For the first time, she wondered why Rachel had not married. She had been the prettier of the two, the more sought-after when they had graduated, a little tardily, from fantasy to real-life dating. A mystery. Had there been more between them than she had realized? Had she ever been physically attracted to Rachel? Her touch had been warm, soft, friendly. But nowhere near as exciting as the touch of Alex, the dreamy-eyed fraternity boy who played the guitar. Or Jay, whom she didn't really like, but who could excite her just by touching her arm, even when she was wearing a long-sleeved dress, a sweater, and a raincoat.

Her mother had often complained that she and Rachel spoke a secret language, that they knew each other so well that they finished each other's sentences. (Laura and Tom, when they were first engaged, had done the same, but her mother had never complained.) The friendship ring — a wide wooden band carved with flowers and leaves — had vanished down the open drain of the sink of Laura's first apartment. When Rachel noticed it was gone, she had stopped wearing hers.

Enough speculation. She returned to the manuscripts. This time she worked on the roman à clef of the failed marriage. Ruthlessly she edited out the author's self-pity, his desire for revenge, his reflections on the nature of relationships between men and women, especially writers and actresses. She wrote crisp cogent comments in the margins. Tonight the ways to make each sentence say what it ought to say seemed to leap from the page. She felt the real story of the novel beginning to stir and come to life.

Perhaps she could ask for an extra manuscript to edit during this week. Better to tidy up someone else's prose than to go through her children's closets. They were old enough to do it themselves when they came home.

As for tidying up her life, there had already been too much of that. Let the clauses dangle for a change, let the modifiers, even the genders, be ambiguous. Pleased with her literary conceit, she returned to her work.

∾ *15* ∾

T HE LETTER FROM TOM arrived on Tuesday morning.
She read it three times that day, once when it first arrived,
once as she sat at her desk trying to work, the third time just
before she went to bed. By then she knew the words almost
by heart.

> Dear Laura,
>
> The phone is no good and there are some things I need to
> say to you before I come home next week. I used to think that
> you would know these things without my saying them, but I
> realize now that this is not so, that people who have been
> married a long time should take nothing between them for
> granted, that it's stupid and even dangerous to do so.

A sudden blurring of the words by her tears. She wiped her
eyes and continued reading.

> I'm still not saying what I mean to say. I'll try again. Laura,
> I love you very much. You are the center of my life, the person
> who gives my work and the rest of my life meaning. This has
> become clear to me since we have been apart. I may not act

very differently when we are back together again, but I wanted you to know.

All my love,
Tom

She carried the letter around with her all day, in the pocket of her bathrobe, of her sundress, in her purse as she left the house for lunch with Lydia, not able — or wanting — to forget about it, not able to respond in any uncomplicated way.

A few months ago she had been parched for signs of affection from Tom, and his words would have brought only joy. Now they brought guilt and confusion as well. The drought was over, but she no longer felt that her entire happiness revolved around whether or not Tom loved her.

The maddening pavan of marriage. As she moved away from him, assuming he wouldn't mind, thinking in fact that he might even welcome it, he moved toward her. As usual, their timing was off.

She had spent the weeks they had been apart exploring aspects of herself long hidden; some, like the attraction to Enid, not even suspected. If she had thought of Tom at all — and he had not often been on her mind in the last few weeks — she had assumed he was a fixed quantity, incapable of change, like a character in a cartoon, condemned to repeat the same gestures again and again.

She tried to remember what he looked like, to picture him in intimate ordinary acts — coming out of the shower, unfolding the *Times,* buttering a piece of toast. Upsetting not to be able to remember one's own husband after an absence of a month and a half.

Distracted in the restaurant, she was startled by the arrival of Lydia, whom she had not seen since the show, although they had spoken on the phone several times. It was through love of Lydia that Laura had taken her first underground journey.

She was wearing not her usual caftan or smock but tight-fitting white pants and a narrow halter that showed off her new slender body. Her hair, which she had always worn loose and unshaped, now framed her face in bouncy becoming curls. Laura was amazed.

"Lydia, what's happened to you? I hardly recognize you. Why, you're beautiful."

Instantly she regretted her words. Surely there was a better way to compliment her friend on the changes in her appearance. But Lydia didn't seem to mind. "Yes, I do look different. Sometimes when I look in the mirror I hardly recognize myself."

During the week of Lydia's show she had sold several paintings, one — the largest and most expensive — to Sam, a lawyer from New Jersey, who had been as attracted to Lydia as to her painting. It was for him she had lost twenty pounds, had her hair cut and curled, bought the sexy new clothes. "Now when I walk into a room, men turn around and stare, just as I've been wishing they would since I was twelve."

"Then what's the problem?" Although Lydia was now much more attractive, in fact looked almost like a different person, she didn't seem much happier.

Lydia shook her head, temporarily interrupted by the waitress returning to ask if they wanted French, Russian, Italian, or house dressing. They chose the house dressing and were told the restaurant was out of it. "That's the problem," Lydia murmured. "Too many people who all seem to want the same thing. What everybody says they want. Intimacy."

She munched mournfully on the mushrooms in her salad. "I thought I did too, but I don't. I know it sounds piggish to complain. But the minute you're alone with them, it doesn't matter whether it's the lawyer from New Jersey, the accountant from Queens, or the artist from the East Village, they always want to know exactly what you're thinking. Especially what you're thinking about them."

She sighed once more, and doused her spinach leaves almost defiantly with more oil than vinegar. Poor Lydia, thought Laura, to get her heart's desire, after all these years, only to find she doesn't want it. Except that it's nice to have the choice, to have, for once, the possibility of rejecting others, instead of being rejected. Laura sensed that Lydia was not as unhappy with her new sense of power as she had said.

Laura felt that the least she could do, in the tradition of the confessional lunch, was to offer a similar experience of her own. She described her Saturday evening with Alan and Enid, each trying to get the other one to leave, each wanting to be alone with her.

Lydia was interested. "Who won?"

"Enid," said Laura, leaving out the last part of the evening, "but only on a technicality. She lives across from the museum, and the electricity was out on the whole block, so she had to stay."

"Not true," reported Lydia, who lived on the same block. Sam and she had stayed in all evening, had not ventured out, in fact, until the next afternoon, because the air-conditioned apartment had been so pleasantly cool. Lydia arose, salad consumed, confessions shared, ready to return to her painting. She gave Laura a sudden shrewd look. "You're sure she told you her apartment had no electricity?"

Laura hedged. "Perhaps I misunderstood." In some ways she liked Lydia better as she had been before the summer. Now that Lydia had eaten from the tree of sexual knowledge, she saw the world more clearly, but less kindly.

As did Laura, and for the same reason. She walked home between large fat drops of warm summer rain, her head full of as much rumbling as the fast-darkening sky. A phrase from Tom's letter echoed along with the thunder. "I may not act very differently."

But they couldn't be the same — too much had happened.

She was no longer the docile timid wife he had left, delighting chiefly in the love of her children and the arrangements of her household. Reciting nightly the prayer, "Don't let my husband leave me. He doesn't have to talk to me, he doesn't have to think about me, just let him stay." She and Tom would have to come to some new agreement; they would have to renegotiate the wedding contract entered into so eagerly and so thoughtlessly twelve years before.

Where would Enid fit into the contract? And Alan? A sudden flash of lightning, a clap of thunder alarmingly close, sent her scudding down the street, blocking out all thought. By the time she reached the lobby of her apartment house she was wet through. And thinking finally about Lydia's inadvertent revelation.

There had been no power failure in Enid's building. Why then had she arrived so disheveled and forlorn, like a stray kitten? Alan wanted his novel published. What was Enid's motive for seduction? Did no one want her for herself alone?

Alan rose from a chair in the lobby, looking as bedraggled as she, although he was completely dry. He had obviously been sitting in the lobby, waiting for her to return since before the rain. Not rain streaks on his cheek then, but tears?

Automatically, maternal words of concern rose to her lips. "Alan, you look awful. What's the matter?"

She took his arm, piloted him protectively into the elevator. Self-protectively also. No good for her reputation as a solid tenant of a solid West End building to have weeping male visitors in the lobby.

She changed quickly from her soggy clothes, set out cookies and iced tea. Not for nothing had she put in long years as comforter of those suffering from bruised knees and shins, or more painful still — and this she guessed to be the case with Alan — from a bruised ego. Noticing that he was not too miserable to eat and drink, Laura sat down beside him and began the final step in the rescue process.

"He's just the first editor, Alan. There are others. I'll make a list for you and you can send it to the next one tomorrow."

He looked at her as if she were a witch, gifted with second sight. "How did you know? I haven't said a word."

"You don't need to. I know the look — first book rejected by first editor. Did he say anything? Did he have any suggestions?"

"He said no. That's all that matters." Alan pulled a crumpled letter from the pocket of his jeans and handed it to her. She smoothed it out until it was readable.

"Why, Alan, this is wonderful. He says it has possibilities."

"But he says it starts too slowly, too awkwardly."

"But look here, he says there are moments of real strength, of tenderness."

"He says it's overwritten."

"He wants to see other things you've done."

They stopped in the middle of their alternating litany of hope and despair. Alan looked at the letter for a long time. "You're right. He did say that. I didn't even see that sentence."

He was hit by another wave of despair, like a swimmer who begins to struggle to his feet and is smacked down by the next giant wave. "He marked up the whole manuscript. He wants me to take out all my favorite parts."

This was going to take longer than she had thought. She was an editor — she should know by now what writers wanted to hear: "It's wonderful — we'll put it on the spring list," or barring that, "It's terrible," so the author could at least think, They don't understand, they've read it all wrong. What no author — especially no beginning author — ever wanted to hear was, "It has possibilities. But it needs work."

"They're probably your favorite parts because they're the parts that really happened. He likes the parts best that you invented."

Alan looked at her with surprise and admiration. "Of course. You're right. And if I invented those, I can invent others." Now the flame of hope was beginning to rekindle. "I didn't see any of those things before. All I could see was that he didn't want to publish it."

As Alan swung up, Laura teetered back toward the ground.

"Have you quit your job yet? Have you said anything to the agency?"

Alan looked sheepish. "Not yet. I didn't quite have the nerve."

Laura stood up, feeling almost like Enid at her most brisk. "Good. Don't. You'll need it for a while longer. But it's time for you to get back to work on your novel."

"Laura, again you've saved my life. And all I've done for you is to make you a Chinese dinner. I'd like to do more." He was recovering rapidly.

She was still being Enid, or perhaps, that part of herself that was most like Enid, the part that liked to take hold of other people's lives and organize them into more meaningful shapes. "Just rewrite. That's the most important thing you can do now."

To herself she sounded fierce, like a WAC sergeant, or an old-fashioned school ma'am. To Alan, astoundingly, she sounded sexually inviting.

"Let me stay here tonight with you, Laura," he pleaded. "After all, it *is* my turn."

He sounded so much like one of her children ("It's not fair, you let *her* do it") that she was not even tempted, had no difficulty propelling him out the door, murmuring in his ear as she closed her door, "Write, Alan. Then call me." No wonder Caroline was so unprofessionally involved with her patient. He was as outrageous as she was.

Alone at last, Laura sagged. Ministering to needy adults was draining. She was beginning to understand Lydia's ambivalence about her social success. There was much to be said for a little psychic distance.

∞ *16* ∞

SHE LAY IN THE TUB, her favorite place for thinking these days, composing letters to Tom in her head. "Dear Tom, I'm not the same person you left at the airport. Will write again when I find out who I've become." "Dear Tom, You'll never guess what I've been doing this summer." "Dear Tom, Your letter saying you still love me has come as quite a surprise . . . "

The only problem was she couldn't possibly send any of them. Perhaps she should cable him the phrase she said so often to the children when she was unwilling to commit herself, "We'll see."

Whatever happened, she appreciated his writing the letter. He had sent his good will and love winging across the ocean, and she was grateful. He was not used to exposing himself so directly, at least not since his ardent wooing on Beacon Hill, and she knew how hard it must have been for him. The question was, had it come too late, after too many years of waning passion, of mutual annoyance and forbearance?

The phone was ringing insistently in the next room. She rose dripping from the tub, wrapped the towel around her body, even though there was no one else in the apartment, and went to answer it.

Enid was calling from Omaha, her presence larger than life, her essence concentrated in the voice in Laura's ear. The words were ordinary — the first lectures had gone well, she was enjoying the books Laura had recommended, she had appreciated Laura taking her in, in her hour of need. Underneath, Laura heard the unasked questions. How was she feeling about their night together, three days later? Were they to continue? If so, on what basis? Unlike Alan, Enid didn't push, but the intensity was there, even stronger for being unspoken. Then the take-over voice she was used to, saying, "Laura, the main reason I called was to tell you about a manuscript buried in the bottom of my bureau drawer. It's a journal I kept when Sarah was very young. The struggle of being both mother and anthropologist, and so forth. It's very rough — I wrote it chiefly to keep myself from going insane. My publisher's been asking to see it for years, but I want you to see it first. Call Edward tomorrow — he's staying at the apartment while I'm away — and he'll find it for you. When I call Thursday you can tell me what you think." Her instructions completed, she hung up.

Laura could no longer continue thinking about Tom. His letter seemed old and faded, as if she had received it many years ago, as a young girl perhaps, not in this morning's mail. Enid's vibrant voice, her demands spoken and unspoken, had taken over the room. Besides, Laura was intrigued with the idea of meeting Edward. She had wondered what kind of man he might be since Enid had first mentioned him.

A gentle, slightly balding man with a paunch. It was clear Edward had never run around Central Park at dawn. She liked him the minute she saw him. He welcomed her into Enid's apartment, asked her to sit down, offered her lemonade. He was obviously used to being accommodating, seemed almost to have made a profession of it.

While he was in the kitchen, Laura walked around the

apartment, looking for signs of Enid's private personality, but there were none. The living room furniture could have come from a Holiday Inn; the bedroom was set up as a study, with file cabinets, bookcases, a studio couch. Sarah's room was equally austere, with no visible toys or stuffed animals. Perhaps they were hidden away in the closet, like Tom's science trophies.

Edward returned to find her peering at the titles in the bookcase. "This isn't really an apartment," he said. "It's a base camp." His tone was factual, unjudgmental. He handed her a glass of lemonade. "I'm glad you're going to edit Enid's manuscript. She writes so well, but she rarely gets around to putting her jottings into publishable form."

She sipped the tart drink (obviously made from real lemons, something she always meant to do, but never did), hearing the implication in his bland words. "I said I would look at the manuscript. I didn't say I would edit it." Actually she hadn't even said she would look at it. Enid had hung up before she could say anything.

Edward immediately apologized. "I'm sorry. I misunderstood. I thought you were interested in the manuscript, interested in Enid."

What had he meant by that remark? She began to feel uneasy, as she did when a salesclerk pushed a product, trying to make her feel guilty for not buying.

Enid had described Edward as a person to whom she had nothing to say, but he seemed very willing to talk to Laura, especially about Enid. "She sounded better last night. I was worried about her when she left. She always gets into a complete panic before she goes off on a lecture tour — sure that no one will come, or if they do, that they'll be bored. Of course it never happens," he said proudly. "She's always a smashing success. But until the first applause, the first question from the audience, she's terrified."

Laura wasn't sure she wanted to hear these revelations. It was almost like stepping through the looking glass to a world where everything was the opposite from the way it seemed on the other side. Edward, however, was eager to continue.

"The worst time is just before she leaves. She's always particularly anxious then, afraid to be alone. Usually that's what she really likes. She rarely seems to need anybody." This last said matter-of-factly, as if he were discussing the changing of the seasons, or the mating habits of the salmon. "I try to stay with her the night before she leaves, but this time I couldn't." He smiled at Laura with a look of gratitude. "I'm so glad you were willing to take her in — to accept her story of the power failure."

Suddenly she felt acutely uncomfortable. He reminded her of Caroline discussing Alan, a parent talking about a beloved but disabled child (particularly beloved, perhaps, because disabled). What, she wondered, is in it for him?

As if reading her thoughts, Edward said, "I suppose you think it's strange that I should still be worrying about my ex-wife. I got into the habit a long time ago, and it's a hard habit to break." His tone was even, friendly, totally devoid of self-pity. "I know Enid's a lesbian now — probably she was when I married her — maybe that's why I did. But she cares for me, no matter what she's told you, and I care for her. Our lives are largely separated now, except for Sarah, but there are still a few things I can do for her."

He went to the other room and returned with a battered manuscript. "Read it, and you'll understand her better. Yourself too, perhaps." He clasped her hand firmly in his "I'm glad to have met you, Laura." He seemed to mean it. "Good luck, whatever you decide to do."

She hurried away with the manuscript in her shopping bag. Edward made her uneasy (that last remark — did it refer to the manuscript or to her relationship with Enid?), but she still liked him. There seemed to be many ways of loving.

∞ *17* ∞

Enid's journal was in almost random order. Several pages were written on the back of a mimeographed lecture on the history of East African fossils. It was as if the author was trying to deny the importance of what she was writing.

Since the entries were dated, it was possible, although difficult, to recreate the sequence. Laura spread out all the pages on the floor of her bedroom, arranging and collating until she had almost a complete manuscript. Then she began to read.

Enid's journal. The struggle of a talented woman to be all the things she wanted to be at the same time. A fine anthropologist, a good wife, a loving mother to a small child. It was impossible, of course; no one could do it, not even Enid, and the pages were filled with the pain of the struggle.

The writing was rough, and there were missing days that would have to be resurrected, but the two sides of Enid — the ambitious professional and the private woman — came through. Both parts real, sometimes working together, sometimes at hopeless odds.

The feeling of triumph when she was chosen "most promising social scientist of the year." The frantic worry when

Sarah had a high fever the day of the presentation, and she and Edward had no sitter they could trust. Edward had stayed home with Sarah. Enid had dashed home after the ceremony to find the fever broken, Sarah's face covered with the blotchy rash of roseola. Also a bottle of orange juice spilled over the only copy of her most recent monograph.

There were odd conjunctions. Sarah's first tooth pushing through the aching baby gums on the same day that Enid identified an ancient incisor. Sarah learning to walk, her first shaky steps observed by her father and a housekeeper in New York, while Enid pored over thigh bones and leg bones in Malaysia, trying to decide if they had or had not come from creatures who could stand erect.

Through it all, utterly, reliable, doing whatever needed to be done, was Edward. Hurrying to Sarah in the middle of the night when she thought she saw a monster in her mirror, comforting Enid when she was sure her facts would be disputed, her theories laughed at. (There was no monster in Sarah's room. Enid's facts were correct. Her theories were accepted by her much older, mostly male, colleagues.)

Laura read for much of the night, scuttling across the rug from one pile of papers to another. Tonight she felt close to Enid, closer even than when they were making love. The only difference between Enid then and Enid now was that today she was more adept at hiding the needy part.

Laura slept through much of the next day, dimly aware of honking horns, pneumatic drills, the aggressive whine of garbage trucks. She was awakened finally by the insidious syrupy melody of the Mr. Softee truck parked at the corner. "It's nothing but chemicals," she had always told the children, hurrying them past the truck. Still the tune buzzed around and around in her head, like a mosquito in the dark. There was only one solution. She slipped off her nightgown, put on her sundress and sandals.

It seemed strange to be standing on a line half a block

from her own apartment. If it had been a Häagen-Dazs line, she would have felt less guilty. But she knew that terrible ice cream, full of chemicals, was what she wanted most at this very minute. After all, she was able to feel all right about sleeping with Enid. Surely she should be able to eat and enjoy a Mr. Softee ice cream cone.

Unlike the experience with Enid, which had not been just a physical craving but the expression of true sharing and friendship, Mr. Softee was a disappointment. The ice cream was both tasteless and too sweet, the cone like soggy cardboard. She walked down the street, licking quickly around the edges of the cone in an unsuccessful attempt to keep the drips from spattering her bare toes. She returned to her apartment, safe at last from temptation, because she had given in to it.

Enid would call tonight. Laura resolved to tell her how reading the journal had made her feel.

The first phone caller was not Enid. It was Jeff, calling excitedly to tell her that he had been selected Camper of the Year. He never thought he would get it, there was going to be a banquet, he would be presented with a silver cup that next year he would hand on to next summer's Camper of the Year. She told him she was delighted, at the same time hoping that the Camper of the Year's mother didn't have to attend the ceremonies. She didn't feel up to another trip to Camp Tumbleweed. An unworthy thought. She definitely did not deserve the Mother of the Camper of the Year Award — at least not this year.

Luckily, Jeff didn't seem to notice her lack of response. "I wrote to Dad," he said, "but he might not get it." Jeff too seemed to feel that Geneva and Tom were far away. "You could tell him when you talk to him."

If I talk to him, Laura thought. She couldn't call Tom until she knew what she wanted to say, and she felt sure he wouldn't call first. She told Jeff she was very proud of him and hung up.

To her surprise, the first thing she said to Enid was, "Guess what. Jeff's been chosen Camper of the Year."

"Oh really?" Was Laura imagining the cool edge in Enid's voice? She had always prided herself on not being one of the mothers who gloated endlessly over the achievements of their offspring, and yet she seemed unable to stop herself.

"You must be very pleased," Enid said. Then, almost without a pause, "Did you read it?" Laura detected a slight quaver. Evidently the needy part of Enid had not gone completely underground.

"I liked it a lot. I read it all night. I couldn't stop."

A sigh of relief across the long-distance wires. "I'm so glad. I wrote it so long ago, I've been almost afraid to look at it. I don't even remember what I wrote."

"We'll have to work on it — there are gaps, repetitions, murky places, but nothing serious. It told me so much about you that I didn't know."

Enid didn't mind personal conversations when she started them. Laura sensed that few people initiated such conversations with Enid, who now quickly changed the subject. "How did you think Edward looked? He's alone so much, I worry about him."

"He was fine. He worries about you, too."

"I know. It's a hard habit to break." Edward's words almost exactly. A long pause. "Did he tell you?"

"About no power failure? He hinted at it. But I knew already."

A long pause. Then a sigh. "I thought he might. I hope you're not angry." Laura realized now that in telling her about Enid's pre-lecture panic, Edward had not been giving away secrets. He was merely doing, as he had always done, what Enid wanted him to do.

"Of course not. Even if I'd known I would have asked you to stay. And I'm glad you did."

"So am I." Another long-distance pause. Laura was beginning to feel as if she were in a Pinter play. "Tell me, what did you think of Edward?" Why did Enid keep talking about Edward? Today Laura was the one moving forward, Enid the one stepping back.

"I liked him. He's a very motherly man."

"Yes," Enid said, almost dreamily, "I've always been attracted to maternal people."

Then abruptly, the brief exposure of the private Enid was over. There were orders to be given, arrangements to be made. "I think the missing parts of the journal are in a folder in the middle drawer of my desk at the museum. I'll call them in the morning and they'll leave a pass for you at the desk. Now I've got to go over my notes for tomorrow's lecture. Graduate students take great pride in asking obscure, intelligent questions. Good night Laura. And thank you."

For what? Laura wondered. For carrying out the royal commands? How did Enid know she didn't have something else to do tomorrow morning? The thought had obviously never occurred to her. She seemed to have Laura mixed up with Edward, the eternally available. She seemed to consider Laura a prime candidate to replace (or perhaps to act as co-director with) Edward in taking care of her.

But Laura wasn't looking for another person to mother. She was Kathy and Jeff's mother. No one else's. Not even Alan's, and in many ways he appealed to her maternal feelings much more than Enid did.

The spasm of anger passed. Just a few nights ago, in this very room Enid had given to Laura as much as she had taken, more in fact. She had made her feel important, valued. Enid gave orders to everybody. That was just her way of talking. Not to everybody did she give a glimpse of the person behind the mask. Laura suspected that Enid had not really forgotten the contents of her journal. She coudn't tell Laura directly, but she very much wanted her to know about those early years, before the woman and the fossil expert had meshed so neatly.

A sudden memory. Laura too had kept a journal during the first year of Jeff's life, daily in the beginning, then weekly. Like a squirrel, pawing through the leaves looking for a special acorn saved for the hour of winter need, she rummaged through the drawers of her desk until she found it, hidden under a thick layer of handmade birthday, anniversary, and Mother's Day cards. She opened the journal and read the first sentences:

> Millions of people have had babies, but this is the first baby on earth as far as we are concerned. I can't believe we really made this total perfect child.

The air-conditioner seemed to be running colder these days, or else the temperature had dropped in the world outside her bedroom. Covering her shoulders with an ancient quilt, she propped the notebook against her knees and prepared to re-enter her own past.

Her journal was very different from Enid's. A detailed chronicle of normal infant development, written as if a series of miraculous events were being described. Jeff's first smile, the first time he responded to his name. Her joy the day that he seemed to recognize an object in a picture book and tried to turn the pages by himself. Tom's excitement the first time Jeff managed to put a plastic ring over the top of a plastic cone.

She wrote about her pleasure at not being pregnant any longer, her delight in Tom's attention to her as well as to the baby. Their eager caresses while they waited for the six-week ban on lovemaking to be lifted. She hadn't been interested in sex the last months — too stuffed full of squirming baby to welcome another intrusion.

Descriptions of Tom cradling Jeff against his shoulder after a feeding, waiting for the mighty burp (so acceptable in infants, so unacceptable in adults). Tom rocking his son during the early evening crying spell, tears streaming down his own cheeks. He had taken his vacation time when Jeff was born, and together they learned how to care for their son. They couldn't afford a nurse and didn't really want one.

At first she had been delighted that she and Tom could be together for such long hours. Then she began to want him to go back to work so she could have the baby to herself. Exulting almost indecently over the long days alone with her child, resenting Tom when he came home and wanted to awaken Jeff so he could play with him. "He treats the baby as if he were a toy, not a real human being." Then no references at all to Tom for months and months. Only the endless list of milestones in the life of the marvelous sweet-tempered babe.

The journal opened a window only into the nursery. Tom had disappeared, but so had she. She had been overwhelmed by the incredible fact that she had created another human being. After the first few weeks she had written as if she had produced Jeffrey entirely by herself, like a queen bee in the hive. But along the way she seemed to have lost her own identity, except as doting mother. Her journal, unlike Enid's, would never interest anybody else. Even she was a little bored reading this meticulously detailed account of the development of a normal baby.

Surely during that year she must have had some thoughts and feelings unconnected with her child. What was it like the first time she and Tom made love after their long abstinence? In the journal only a record of the great day, or great night, at almost two months, when Jeff slept through for the first time. "It feels so wonderful to be sleeping six hours without interruption." How had she felt picking up a wet, crying baby at two or three o'clock every night for two months? Had she really been filled with tender loving feelings every time?

If there had been ambivalence (and even now she could not remember any), it did not appear in the pages of her journal. This had been a time of great happiness for her, of great emotional intensity.

And, she suddenly realized, a time of shutting out as well as embracing. Her love affair with her baby son had been the beginning of the end of her love affair with Tom. She had wished him gone so that she could have this new male child they had created together all to herself. So she could hug him and tend him, and look upon his naked, infant, but distinctly male body with pleasure.

She had felt so smug and self-righteous during the days when she had been convinced that Tom was interested in someone else. She had thought, How can he? I would never do a thing like that to him.

Now, rereading her journal of ten years ago, she knew better. She had done it first.

∞ *18* ∞

THAT NIGHT A DELUGE. Flashes of lightning visible even through the shades, claps of thunder like bombs going off, then an angry distant rumble. She walked through the rooms of the apartment closing windows, pursued everywhere by the flashes and the noise.

No children to comfort, to say, "It's all right. It's just a summer storm. The rain will be good for the flowers." Actually, neither child was afraid of electric storms. They liked the drama, the display. Awakened by thunder, they usually arose, pulled up their shades to watch, and would have run downstairs in their nightclothes if she had let them. She was the one storms always made uneasy, even in a city apartment, surrounded by concrete and insulation.

Laura counted the seconds between flash and crash. That's what her father had called it — he had taught her how to calculate how close the lightning was when she was six years old, and had rushed into her parents' bedroom in terror. Still very close. She put her head under the covers, breathed deeply until the intervals began to lengthen (like the rhythm of labor pains, except then the intervals came closer and closer).

Strangely enough, she had not been frightened during

labor. Both times she had been exhilarated (the second not as much as the first), feeling herself at the center of an exciting natural phenomenon, her own personal earthquake. A process unstoppable once it had begun, but not frightening because she had planned it, she wanted it, and because it would bring forth a living child.

Anxious about much, she had never doubted that her child would be born whole, healthy, perfect. Much more chance of birth trauma, lack of oxygen, a cord wrapped around the baby's neck at the last second, than of being struck by lightning. But then fears were not based on statistical probabilities.

Only faraway rumblings now, and the heavy pounding of the rain on the air-conditioner. In her dreams the sound was transformed into the rocking of a cradle, back and forth, back and forth, but whose hand rocked the cradle and who lay passive, being rocked, she didn't know.

Waking, lying in bed, not yet ready to start the day, she thought about the image in her dream. Even among adults, it seems, there were the mother and the mothered. With Alan it was obvious, with Enid less evident but equally true. They both hoped she would take care of them. She sighed as she thought about this.

Not really the emergence of a new, adventurous personality after all. Just the same old one in disguise. Was she never to put aside her maternity clothes ("eternity clothes" a friend had once called them) and come forth as herself?

Only Tom had not wanted to make her into his mother. Once they had taken care of each other. For a long time he had not asked anything from her at all. Except that she go with him to Geneva. And now the letter, with its tacit plea.

All day as it continued to rain, Laura was haunted by memories of the past, the past that she and Tom had shared, the parts that had been left out of the journal.

In the afternoon she went to the museum. The rest of Enid's manuscript was in the middle drawer of her desk, as she had said. Strange to be in Enid's office when she was not there. Laura scooped up the papers and left quickly, not sure she wanted to stir up the image of Enid today.

Instead, she went to visit the exhibit of minerals, gems, and meteorites. Here it was dark, almost deserted, and she could wander from one lighted case to the next, looking at tourmalines, sapphires, amethysts, jade, while a soothing educational voice recited facts about the wonderful world that lay beneath the surface of the earth.

For over an hour she wandered in the cave of the jewels, passing some cases two and three times. As she moved through the carpeted labyrinth of steps and passageways, she ran movies in her head of her early life with Tom. The two of them doing errands together on Saturday mornings, then carrying their purchases up the four flights to their first apartment, the one on Seventeenth Street with the slanted floor. (Once she spilled a carton of orange juice, and it ran all the way to the front door.) Cooking together for their friends, washing the dishes in the minuscule sink. Lying in bed on Sunday mornings making love, doing the crossword puzzle together, getting up finally to shower, soaping each other's slippery bodies in the most private places, sometimes then, roused by their water play, making love once more on the unmade bed. Driven at last by hunger out into the streets in search of croissants and coffee. Pausing in the sunshine to listen to the musicians around the fountain in Washington Square, to look at the paintings of sunsets and children with enormous eyes in the Greenwich Village Art Show.

Eventually they'd arrive at the Eighth Street Bookstore, there to separate for the first time since Friday night. She browsing among the poetry, the novels, the collections of short stories. He inspecting books on history, sociology, science; sometimes even, she suspected, taking furtive glances at the sex manuals and the books of nude photographs.

In bookstores they always separated. If they passed each other between tables of discount books, they nodded briefly, impersonally, as if to a casual acquaintance. They came together again at the cash register, as if by prearranged signal. But by then their minds had separated also. It was now Sunday night and they needed to get ready for their largely separate weeks, he as a very junior chemist in a large firm, she as a first reader at Wickerson and Lowe.

Flashback to Boston, the apartment on Mt. Vernon Street. Fourth floor again. There was the magnificent view of the roofs and chimneys of the back of Beacon Hill. She and Tom curled up in an enormous sagging armchair, kissing. Her roommates returned in the early dusk, bringing pizza, wine, and other people. They had blinked in surprise when the lights came on.

Tom had risen only to bring her wine and feed her pizza as if she were too delicate to get up and fetch her own food. In these days he hovered over her protectively. When he couldn't take her to her door, he always insisted that she call him as soon as she got home. And she, infected by his concern, was not completely at ease until she had let him know that once again she had arrived uninjured.

"Excuse me, lady. Could you move a little? The children want to see the petrified wood."

She turned, startled to see a short red-faced man surrounded by a large group of boys all wearing shorts, baseball caps, and T-shirts emblazoned with the words Camp Pioneer. It must still be raining, she thought. The counselors are desperate. Having already seen the dinosaurs, the hall of the mammals, the giant whale, they've brought them all here to look at rocks.

It was time for her to leave, but now that she wanted to go, she couldn't seem to find the exit. She circled the exhibit several times, always returning, against her will, to the central carpeted stairs where children were now practicing jumps, somersaults, handstands, while their counselors threatened expulsion, excommunication, deprival of snacks and souvenirs. Had she been condemned to spend the rest of her life wandering in the dark among ancient rocks and restless campers?

Beginning to feel trapped, she looked for a museum guard, but they were all hiding. Perhaps she should have left a trail of crumbs, like Hansel and Gretel, although the campers would probably have eaten them. On her fourth trip around the circle she came upon the way out, almost blocked by incoming children. She hurried down the corridor leading toward the light, through the Biology of Man, past the giant Indian canoe and the souvenir counter where children were pushing and shoving each other, and out the side door to Seventy-seventh Street. She blinked in the bright sunshine that had supplanted the rain. She had been so immersed in the past that she had expected to emerge into the Boston of over a decade ago.

Suddenly she knew that she would go to Boston. She would go today. There it would be easier to remember Tom as he had been in their early courtship days. There, also, she would track down her pre-Tom self. The person she had been before she began to perceive life as a series of items on a list.

If only she could be instantly transported, without the bother of calling Amtrak, making hotel reservations, packing her suitcase, calling Camp Tumbleweed. But there was no help for it. She didn't believe in telekinesis. And there was no time to lose. Tom would be back in a few days. She hurried to Broadway and leaped on the first uptown train.

∽ *19* ∽

SHE WAS IN THE MIDST of tucking rolled-up underpants and stockings into the corners (it seemed like only a few days ago that she had packed for Tom) when the phone rang. Caroline announced triumphantly that George and Sandra had separated, or rather that Sandra had left, leaving George with the baby, the parakeet, and the Labrador retriever. Why, Laura wondered, does Caroline take such pleasure in each breakup? Aren't therapists supposed to be in favor of people staying together? Perhaps it makes her feel less lonely to realize that other people's lives are no more secure than her own constantly shifting arrangements.

Amazingly, Caroline didn't seem to know about Laura and Enid. Her antennae picked up, however, when Laura said she couldn't meet her at St. Mark's for a poetry reading (two of her ex-patients were on the program — a therapeutic and artistic triumph), because she was going to Boston.

"Boston? Why there? Isn't Tom due back next week?" Caroline seemed able to keep track of the schedules of her friends, as well as those of her patients.

"I'd rather not say. It's personal," Laura said and hung up, leaving Caroline, she hoped, panting with curiosity.

She hurried down the steps to the subway platform, her suitcase hitting each step behind her. What had possessed her to pack so much — manuscripts, most of the clothes she had bought this summer, the black satin nightgown Tom had bought for her birthday two years ago that she had not yet worn? Even a folding umbrella, although there was now not a cloud in the sky. In this weather, all she really needed was a pair of sunglasses and a bikini.

If she hurried, she would have just enough time to catch the five-fifteen. At the bottom of the stairs she almost bumped into a large black man who was weeping as if his heart would break. The crowds of people going up and down paid no attention to him beyond parting slightly on either side, like the waters of the Red Sea.

She too was about to move past, keeping a few inches to the right so that she would not touch him by mistake, and possibly change his grief to an equally mysterious rage. But something in the quality of his crying made her stop.

She placed her suitcase between her body and the side of the stairway, so that it could not easily be taken from her, and bent over him. "Is something the matter?" An idiotic question.

He raised his streaming eyes, then shook his head, whether to say yes or no it was hard to say. Tears continued to pour down his cheeks.

She tried again. "Can I help you in some way? Where are you going? Are you waiting for a train?"

To all her questions, he shook his head, seeming not to understand. A woman coming-up behind her suggested, "Maybe he doesn't speak English."

A sudden surge of passengers pressed forward against them, trying to make their way upward to the street. "Hey, lady," an angry commuter in a hurry yelled, jabbing Laura in the ribs with his attaché case, "This is a helluva place to hold a conversation."

Agreeing, she retrieved her suitcase. Holding the man by the elbow, the woman on his other side, they propelled him down the stairs and onto a bench. He was surprisingly easy to move, his huge body offering no resistance.

Something about the look in his eyes was familiar — almost the way Jeff had looked when he was three and had gotten separated from her in the supermarket. Of course. She should have realized it at once, but she had been distracted by the adult body. A lost child. He was probably mentally retarded.

By now a small group of people had gathered around the bench. They stood back respectfully as Laura leaned forward to ask her next question. "Can you tell me your name? Or where you live?" She noticed that his legs were trembling. He was as frightened as Jeff had been when she had finally found him in the manager's office. She touched his hand. "Don't worry. Everything's going to be all right."

At that minute, a young man with a green bookbag and matching sneakers stepped forward. "I think I know who he is. I've seen him on Broadway, near Eighty-sixth. His name is Calvin. Or is it Luther?" He grinned down at the older man, who smiled back. "Anyway, one of those Reformation names."

A transit policeman broke through the edge of what was now a small crowd. Where has he been all this time? Laura wondered. He seemed to know the man on the bench very well. He took him by the arm and began to lead him toward the stairs just as a very old, very small black woman came hurtling down.

"Sonny," she screamed, "where've you been? You had me scared out of my wits."

It was time for Laura to leave. An emergency might bring New Yorkers together temporarily. But as soon as it was over, it was necessary to sever the connection, and proceed as if nothing had happened. With barely perceptible gestures of farewell, Laura and the woman and the young man with a bent for history parted from each other.

She missed her train and had to take a local that seemed to stop at every town between New York and Boston. It was almost midnight when she arrived at the Copley Plaza, the only hotel she remembered, the one where she and Tom had stayed on their wedding night.

She fell asleep immediately, as if she were entering a tunnel. This time, when she emerged from darkness into light, she was indeed in Boston.

∞ *20* ∞

ANOTHER FRIDAY NIGHT alone in Geneva. It seemed to Tom that he had been on his own for at least a decade, looking for ways to fill up his time, and trying to keep from worrying about what was happening on the other side of the Atlantic.

Mr. Torval had left, but Professor Ulrich had asked if Tom could stay on until Tuesday. He wanted to discuss the possibility of Tom's giving a seminar at the University of Geneva next summer. Tom had said of course he could stay, but tonight Tuesday seemed a long way off.

No answer yet to his letter to Laura. He tried not to think about what that might mean. Well, at least he could talk to her tonight. Their usual Friday night phone call. The weekly call that had become more and more remote — almost worse than not talking to each other at all.

There was only one way for them to talk. In person. Why should he wait until next week when he wanted so very much to see Laura now? He would leave a note for Professor Ulrich saying he had been called home unexpectedly. He could deal with the problem of the seminar later. Tonight he would leave for New York. It would be romantic to arrive just as Laura was waking. He would tell her that he couldn't wait another minute to be with her.

Luckily the company travel agent was still in the hotel, making arrangements for the last of the conference members. As Tom began hastily piling his clothes into his suitcase, dirty laundry and all, he realized that it was the first time in many years that he had packed a suitcase for himself.

The minute he stepped out of the air-conditioned terminal at Kennedy, he was wrapped in a heavy blanket of foul-smelling air. He decided to take a taxi into Manhattan. It would bring him to Laura more quickly.

At the corner of Broadway where the taxi let him out, the neighborhood plant store was just opening for business. The bunches of flowers outside on the sidewalk were still covered with large shimmering drops of water. He bought six roses, three red and three yellow.

Halfway down the block he began to feel uneasy. Perhaps he should have called first. Maybe they were too old for romantic surprises. Laura might not be ready to have her summer privacy intruded upon.

That was ridiculous. It was his apartment too. Surely he didn't have to make an appointment to enter it.

He let himself in with his house key, noticing that the *Times* was still on the doormat. Laura was still asleep then. It was not part of his plan to frighten her. He decided to make fresh coffee and bring it to her in bed.

He had forgotten that the electric dripolator took so long to go through its noisy cycle. He tiptoed down the hall to their bedroom, coffee cup in hand. One teaspoon of sugar, no cream, just the way Laura liked it.

The door was open, and he could see at once that no one was in the bed. The bedspread was still pulled smoothly over the pillows. He stood on the threshold, flabbergasted. This was a possibility he had never considered. Where could Laura be? Had something happened to her?

He prowled through the rooms, looking for clues. The apartment was hot and airless, all the windows closed — a sign that Laura had not just stepped out on an early morning errand. Anyway, what kind of errand would bring Laura out of the house before eight o'clock? She was not a morning person.

The bulletin board was empty, except for a typed list of cities (Palo Alto, Ann Arbor, Kansas City) with dates and phone numbers, on stationery from the American Museum of Natural History. They had not been to the museum for many years, not since the days when they used to take the children there on Sunday afternoons. What did the list mean?

In the dining room, under the Gro-Lite, the plants were thriving. He touched his finger to the soil. Slightly damp. Laura could not have been gone for very long. A plant he had never seen before, a lush jungly-looking flower with spiked leaves, the pot covered in shiny red foil. Obviously a present — a small card was still taped to its side.

Shamelessly he read it. "To Laura from Alan. For saving my life — again." Despite the heat, a shiver went down his spine.

A sudden premonition sent him to the bathroom. Yes. Her toothbrush was gone, also her hairbrush and deodorant. He hurried to the closet. Laura's clothes stared back at him, keeping their owner's secret. When had she bought that purple dress? And that polka dot halter? He turned on the closet light and peered at the shelves over the clothes rod.

Laura's plaid suitcase was gone, the boxes and pocketbooks tumbling forward in a heap. He began to look around the bedroom, like Sherlock Holmes. A number of signs indicated that she, who was always so deliberate, had left in a hurry. One sandal on a chair, two blouses on the top of the bureau, the manuscripts on her desk tipping perilously close to the edge.

For a long time he sat on a corner of the bed, wondering what he should do. Finally he decided to call Lydia. She might know where Laura was, or at least, where she might be.

Lydia sounded half-asleep. Like most people who have been awakened by the telephone, she denied that she had been sleeping. "Tom," she said, struggling to remember who he was, then suddenly remembering. "What's the matter? I thought you were still in Geneva."

"I came home a few days early. Laura's not here. Do you have any idea where she is?"

There was a long pause at the other end of the phone, the sound of a whispered conversation. For the first time it occurred to him that Lydia might have someone in bed with her. Her voice again, now fully awake. "No, none. But I'm sure there's nothing wrong. She's probably gone away for the weekend. Anybody would, if they could."

He had not said he was worried about where Laura was. Why had she been so quick to reassure him? He realized that Lydia was still talking. "After all, Tom, she didn't expect you."

It was obvious she hadn't. He put down the phone, wondering whom he could call next. On a small note pad next to the phone he noticed two lines in Laura's handwriting, "Penn Station 5:15," and a telephone number with an area code.

For a long time he hesitated about whether to call the number. Suppose a man answered — what would he say then? "Please return my wife. I need her." He decided to take the chance. With great relief, after several rings, he heard the voice of a hotel clerk with an obvious Boston accent. "Copley Plaza. May I help you?" Yes, they had a Mrs. Stone registered, a Mrs. Laura Stone. Again an involuntary shiver, as he suffered the uncoupling of his first name. No, Mrs. Stone was not in just now. Would he care to leave a message? Tom left their home number, asking her to call as soon as she got in.

He called several times in the afternoon, but she was still not there. What could she be doing that would keep her out all day? Whenever they had traveled together she wanted to go back to the hotel and rest before any afternoon excursion. "Just to touch base," she always said.

He dozed between phone calls, waking in late afternoon to realize he was very hungry. In the refrigerator he found only a container of plain yogurt and a box of slightly mouldy strawberries.

He was afraid to leave the house lest he miss her call. He finally made himself a peanut butter sandwich from the dry remnants in the bottom of a huge jar of Mr. Planter. The children often ate peanut butter sandwiches unaccompanied by any liquid. How did they do it? The peanut butter stuck firmly to the roof of his mouth, and for a long panicky moment until he took a gulp of water, he felt he might never be able to swallow again.

Laura seemed to have lost interest in food for herself. Had she at least remembered to leave food for Harold? He hurried to Jeff's room.

Harold had vanished without a trace. Along with his cage, his wheel, and the cardboard tunnel that Jeff had made for him from the middle of a roll of paper towels. It was as if the hamster had never existed.

An almost engulfing wave of self-pity. Is that what would happen to him and all of his possessions, if Laura should decide that she no longer wanted him?

Jet lag must really be getting to him. Whatever happened next, he would need to be in better shape than this when she called. Cool, rational, and understanding, no matter what she said.

He went into the bathroom, shaved, and showered. In the foyer he found the *Times*, his luggage, and the roses of the morning, now completely wilted. He turned on the air-conditioner and began to read. It was almost seven o'clock when he was awakened by the ringing of the phone.

He leaped forward and caught it before the second ring. "Laura," he shouted hoarsely into the mouthpiece, "what are you doing in Boston?"

∞ *21* ∞

ON BEACON HILL THE GOLDEN DOME of the State House glittered in the morning sun the way she remembered it. Louisburg Square was still surrounded by elegant nineteenth-century townhouses with fan-shaped glass above their heavy front doors and shiny brass knockers. The cobblestones pressed through the soles of her sandals as she looked at a place where nothing had changed.

She climbed the steep slope of Mount Vernon Street. She peered up at the windows of the room where she and Tom had first begun to explore each other, while her roommates slept in the crowded bedroom next door. The windows were now covered with heavy wooden shutters, not with the fishnet that they had so enthusiastically and cavalierly stapled to the window frames.

∞∞∞

In those days, she had slept in the living room because she was the first to get up. Hurrying down the not-so-beautiful back of Beacon Hill in the early morning chill, she had run for an eight o'clock train to Winchester. There, in the only office building in town, she and Mr. Richardson, a quiet scholarly man who always gave her exact change whenever he took a stamp from the office stamp box, edited a small, worthy, and very nonprofit magazine, *Education for Better Living*. Its only subscribers were university libraries and foundations.

There were no trains returning to Boston in the late afternoon, only the shop train from the railroad yards at Billerica. Mr. Richardson arranged for the train to pick her up in a brief screeching halt at the Winchester station.

The men, exhausted by their day's work in the yards, never looked at her. They dozed, or played cards in the double facing seats at the back of the car. Laura sat beside the only other female on the train, a middle-aged woman named Mary who worked in the office at the yards. They did not speak (Laura feeling that she should wait for the older woman to make the first move) until the July afternoon when she boarded the train wearing her brand-new engagement ring.

Mary had noticed the ring immediately, beamed her approval, then asked when she was getting married. From then on she spoke to Laura every day. She chatted about her work in the yards ("Don't let the men scare you. They talk rough sometimes, but they're a good bunch"), her life at home with her husband ("A good man even if he does drink too much"), her children and grandchildren.

With her acquisition of the ring, Laura's status automatically changed from nonexistent person to member of the female club. Even the pretty young checker at the supermarket noticed and offered congratulations. Sometimes Laura felt as if she were wearing a blinding headlight on her left hand, instead of a tiny diamond chip. But she had been too excited about her coming marriage to be intimidated by the attention of strangers. As when she was pregnant, it never crossed her mind that the marriage might not be happy, healthy, perfect.

‿‿‿

Now Laura walked up and down the slanting streets, looking for buildings where friends had lived, trying to remember who had lived where and with whom. She inspected the windows of basement and first-floor apartments, a habit that had always annoyed Tom. She was a respecter of privacy but even stronger was her desire to see how other people arranged their rooms.

She looked in the windows of antique stores (many more than there had been, or had she just never noticed them — not then so preoccupied with the past?), the used-book stores, the laundromats. No memory of ever having entered one. What had she done with her dirty clothes?

Here and there were signs about apartments for rent. "USE OF GARDEN. SEE SUPER." Laura had never lived in an apartment with a garden. In fact, she had never lived in an apartment by herself. First with her parents, then her roommates, then Tom.

Sitting in the Public Garden, munching a hot dog bought from a passing vendor (another food she had always cautioned the children against), she looked at the real estate section of the *Boston Globe*. "Two rooms with bath. Working fireplace." "Top floor of townhouse. Private entrance, original parquet floors."

She began to decorate the rooms, place small Oriental rugs on the floors, move her books into the built-in bookcases, perhaps even rent a spinet for the corner. She waters the plants, plays a little Bach on the piano. She sketches the view of the Common through the many-paned bow window across the front room.

She is wearing a long black velvet skirt, a white silk blouse with a ruffle at the throat. She is lighting candles, drawing the curtains. People are coming for tea or dinner — literate, intelligent, appreciative people. Someone (the face, even the sex, is unclear) lingers after the others have gone to discuss the party, the state of the nation, the state of the arts.

Then Laura remembered. She could cease to be a wife, but not cease to be a mother. Clattering up the stairs of her mind comes Kathy with three friends, all wearing Girl Scout uniforms. They head for the kitchen where they will want to bake massive quantities of brownies. Jeff enters, followed by the members of his rock band, planning a rehearsal in the living room. Enter reality. Exit gracious living, at least for quite a while.

Laura was not altogether unhappy to see it go. She was no Emily Dickinson, although like most women, there were days when she yearned to put on a white dress and refuse to come downstairs. Even Emily, she imagined, would not have wished to live in a house where there was no downstairs, where the room with the desk and the ink and paper was all there was.

She did not actually crave complete solitude or continuous elegance. Just occasional doses of each. But suppose no one stayed after the others went home, or wanted to stay? Suppose there was no one special person?

She remembered Tom, breathless at the door of her Mount Vernon Street apartment, trying to see how far he could get before the heavy oak door downstairs clicked shut. "Third floor this time. I'll make it yet," he said when his breath came back, his arms tight around her. Tom waiting as she stepped off the dusty shop train in North Station, telling her he loved her over stale Danish and tepid coffee in the station coffee shop. He shouldn't have been there. He should have been studying for exams, but he said he couldn't get through a day without seeing her.

Laura folded the real estate section and dropped it into the nearest trash basket. The time for living alone gracefully on Beacon Hill, if it had ever existed, was long past.

She decided to spend the rest of the afternoon looking for something special to give Tom when she saw him again. She walked up and down Newbury Street looking in shop windows at leather goods, neckties, cuff links. Eventually she found what she wanted in a small gift shop near the Copley — an expensive Swiss watch called Le Jour Chronograph. It showed speed as well as minutes, seconds, and fifths of seconds. It could be used as a stopwatch; it gave the date; it was shock resistant and self-winding. She didn't know why it was in an ordinary gift shop among the perfumes and scarves and boxes of chocolates, but she knew that Tom would love it, and that she wanted very much to give it to him. He might already have bought a watch in Geneva, but she guessed he hadn't. Tom rarely felt justified in buying for himself things he really wanted.

She knew she didn't want to present it to him in their apartment, filled with memories of their domestic life and of her summer alone. They needed to meet in a place that belonged only to the two of them. Where their past was still visible. Impulsively, she sent a cable to Tom's hotel in Geneva.

PLEASE CHANGE AIR TICKETS FROM NEW
YORK TO BOSTON. MEET ME IN THE PUB-
LIC GARDEN NEAR SWAN BOATS, SUNDAY 3
P.M. LOVE, LAURA.

She called the hotel desk and asked for a double room for Sunday night. One in front, if possible, with plenty of light. "My husband will be joining me," she told the clerk. "He's flying in from Geneva."

She wanted to hear the desk clerk murmur, perhaps with a touch of envy, "How nice for you," but she was asked only, "Twin beds or a double?"

As soon as the arrangements were made (she was becoming very good at making arrangements), Laura was filled with doubts. Would it be nice for her? They had been apart for almost two months. She could now remember Tom's Boston face, it's true, but it would be his older, closed-off New York face he would be bringing with him. How would her new self fit with her old husband?

There was an urgent knocking at the door. The bellboy handed her what looked like a mountain of pink telephone slips, all with the same message: "Call your husband in New York as soon as possible." It had not occurred to her to ask at the desk for messages. No one except the director of Camp Tumbleweed knew she was here.

As she searched frantically in her bag for a tip for the bellboy, her heart began to pound. Something dreadful must have happened.

$\sim$ *22* $\sim$

SHE DIALED HER HOME NUMBER with trembling fingers. The phone rang once, then Tom's voice, angry, accusing. "Laura, what are you doing in Boston?"

She could answer only with other questions. "What are you doing in New York? Has something happened? Are the children all right?"

The children. Always the children. Didn't Laura ever think about him? Maybe there was something wrong with him. Except, of course, there wasn't. Nothing physical, that is.

"No, nothing's wrong with the children. At least, nothing that I know about. But you haven't answered my question. Why aren't you here, in the apartment?"

Where you belong. She could hear the end of the sentence as clearly as if Tom had said it aloud. They had reached a conversational stalemate with remarkable speed. Was this the man to whom she had just sent a loving cable, asking him to speed across the Atlantic to her side?

It was, after all, a reasonable question. And now that she tried to answer it honestly, a very difficult one. Her reasons for coming, the reasons why she *had* to come, had seemed much clearer on Friday night, clearer even a few minutes ago. She took a deep breath and tried.

"I wanted to see Boston again, the place where we first met, the place where I used to live before I met you." She could not help adding, "And I didn't expect you until next week."

Why did everybody keep reminding him? He felt like an actor stumbling on stage before his cue. "I came home early because I couldn't wait until next week. I wanted to see you right away." A long pause. He replayed what she had just said — her reasons for going to Boston. So she too had been thinking about their past.

Surprisingly, Laura began to giggle, a light girlish laugh that he hadn't heard in a long time. "It's really funny, Tom. You were rushing to New York to be with me. And I just sent a cable to Geneva, asking you to meet me here, tomorrow afternoon."

"Where?"

"In the Public Garden, near the swan boats. At three o'clock."

A feeling of tremendous relief. He felt jubilant, lightheaded, as if he had been drinking champagne. "I'll be there. On the dot."

He had almost asked, "But how will I recognize you?"

On Sunday it occurred to Laura that it might be raining in the Public Garden. Perhaps she should not have chosen an outdoor site for their reunion. It had not been raining in any of the scenes in her slide show of the past, but just in case she put the folding umbrella into her canvas bag along with a manuscript.

She was sitting on a park bench opposite the swan boats at a little after two-thirty. Too nervous to read, even to think. Best to try to stay calm, to relax, to let whatever was going to happen happen. She tried repeating to herself the advice she had given so glibly to the frightened man in the subway. "Don't worry. Everything will be all right."

She felt as though she were going to meet a stranger. More excited than when she waited for Alan, than when she had danced with Enid.

What should she tell Tom when he asked, as he surely would, whom she had been seeing in New York, what she had been doing? The conventions of their world were curious. Her body had not been suspicious of her growing desire for Enid. Tom's jealousy would not be aroused by her having a new friend who was a woman. All of the facts (or most of them) innocuous sounding, unthreatening to his male ego: the mother of a friend of Kathy's, an anthropologist, a writer whose journal she was going to edit.

Alan, however, was immediately suspect. She could hear Tom now. "You drove up to camp with him, you read his novel, you slept in the same bed with him, and you expect me to believe it was nothing?" Not nothing exactly, but nothing for Tom to worry about, although she couldn't blame him for not seeing it this way. About Enid she was not so sure.

Only one thing was she sure about. Any two people who lived together for a long time worked out arrangements that suited them both, whether they knew it or not. She and Tom had needed to pull back for a while, to retire to their respective marital corners. But now it was time to see if it was possible for them to come back together.

Usually Tom was comfortable on a plane. He liked the feeling of being away from the earth, away from telephones, memos, obligations. It was one of the few times he allowed himself to relax, to daydream, to think about things that were not connected with his daily schedule.

Not so today. Laura's behavior had been uncharacteristic. She liked plans to be made well in advance. Like most dedicated worriers, she was against spontaneity on principle. Or so he had thought.

It had never occurred to him not to meet Laura in Boston.

The command had come and he had obeyed. And now he was being transported to an assignation in the Public Garden.

It had been while riding in a swan boat that Laura had said she would marry him. Her words had made him incredibly happy. He had felt as if he could leap out of the boat and propel it forward with the force of his joy. Only one other time could he remember being so happy — when Jeff was born.

Now, at the dinner table, the children's chatter drowned out all adult conversation. Not that they had much conversation to drown. The minute he walked in the door Laura wanted him to look at the vacuum cleaner, which was making that funny noise again. Or Kathy had been squinting lately, did he think they should have her eyes checked?

What had they talked about in their courtship days? They used to spend hours on the phone, even when they had been together all day. Talking so long that his ear was sore when he finally put down the receiver.

He and Laura seemed to have lost their delight in each other's company. And then had come Amy, bringing him the excitement of an unknown body and personality, the sweet feeling of being needed. She had brought also lessons in the strategy of deceit, the agony of indecision and guilt. Although he was sure Laura still didn't know.

As he didn't know what she had been doing this summer, and with whom. Who was Alan? And why did his life need saving so many times? There was a lot he didn't know about the person who would be waiting by the swan boats. It was disturbing. He glanced at his watch. If the plane landed on time, he would just have time to grab a cab and meet Laura.

She was standing by the edge of the pond, just as she had been on that Sunday afternoon thirteen years ago. Her hair was shorter now, her figure a little less willowy, but she was clearly the same person. But why was she carrying an umbrella? The sky was bright blue without a cloud. Absurd for her to be so cautious. She was surely not so cautious then. Suddenly Laura caught sight of him and opened the umbrella, twirling it flirtatiously in his direction, as if it were a parasol and she a Renoir woman strolling in the Bois de Boulogne.

A tall thin man hurrying across the Public Garden, seriously impeded by a suitcase and a briefcase. For heaven's sake, why hadn't Tom checked his luggage at the airport? Did he think it was his clothes she had missed? Now he had seen her and, despite his burdens, began to run. She closed the umbrella and moved quickly toward him.

∽ *23* ∽

AFTER THE FIRST INTENSE EMBRACE, they drew back, almost as if embarrassed. They were like invalids recovering from the flu, not wanting to do too much on the first day. They inquired about each other's journeys to Boston. They exchanged anecdotes about eccentric fellow passengers. The man sitting next to Tom playing solitaire who, after three martinis, loudly accused himself of cheating. The woman on the train with three children under seven, trying to pretend they were somebody else's, keeping her eyes closed even while they climbed into her lap and rummaged in her pocketbook.

Tom opened his briefcase, took out a small package and thrust it at Laura, like a fifteen-year-old presenting his first corsage. She unwrapped it slowly, found a thin gold chain, a tiny delicate flower encased in a chip of lucite.

"It's edelweiss, the Swiss national flower. It grows in the Alps," he said, sounding like the educational voice in the museum. His voice trembled a bit. "Do you like it?"

"Like it? I love it. It's beautiful. Here, help me put it on." In the desert, in the Alps, small delicate flowers manage to grow, despite many obstacles.

Tom was equally pleased with his watch, more so perhaps since he had not been expecting a present.

They deposited Tom's luggage in a locker at the bus station in Park Square, returned to the Garden to take a ride in a slow-moving swan boat. Even a real swan moved faster. Tom reminded her that she had accepted his proposal in a swan boat. She was glad that he remembered.

"Let's go look at the apartment," she said, taking Tom's hand and leading him up Beacon Hill to the building where he had charged up the stairs. Tom's memory of the event was different. It was not here, he insisted, but in their first apartment in New York, on Seventeenth Street, that he had been so athletic. Laura was sure he was wrong. The image of Tom racing up the stairs to reach her was one of her clearest memories of their courtship.

"Remember the first dinner you cooked for me here? You couldn't figure out how to light the oven, but you wouldn't admit it. I thought all you were going to serve me was cheese and crackers."

Here Laura's memory was blank. "That never happened. Or if it did, it was only for a few seconds."

Tom laughed and put his arm around her. "The longest first course I ever had." Unfair of him to remember what she had so conveniently forgotten.

They decided to look for the coffee shop where Tom had first asked Laura to marry him ("Let me think about it," she had said). Tom thought it had been on Joy Street. She was sure it had been Willow. They found it on Myrtle, a few streets below the State House, but so changed that it was almost unrecognizable. It was now a small restaurant filled with leafy plants, an exposed brick wall, and a menu featuring quiche, omelets, and strawberry-yogurt pie. It could easily have been the Museum Café, except they seemed to be the only customers over thirty. They were surrounded by groups of students, laughing, talking eagerly. Tom showed her a white-haired couple in a corner booth. Laura said, "Yes, but they're wearing T-shirts and jeans. Maybe we should have eaten at the Copley."

Tom pointed out that they would have been even more out of place at the Copley café. He remembered that she was always uneasy, no matter where she was. She remembered how much he liked to be right.

The minute they entered the lobby of the Copley, she realized that this time he had been. Alone, she had not looked at the other guests. Now she saw that everyone was middle-aged, affluent, their luggage made of leather not nylon, some bags even with gold or hand-stitched initials. There seemed to be no one in Boston who was just like them. Everyone seemed to have just met or to have known each other all their lives.

Upstairs in their bedroom they undressed quickly, silently. Almost as if they had no right to be there, as if, if they made any noise, they would be thrown out by the rightful occupants of the room, the couple on their honeymoon twelve years before. They were both tired. Neither of them had slept much the night before, and Tom had been traveling for two days.

Laura slipped the black nylon nightgown over her head. The material clung to her hips and breasts like the hands of a lover. She wondered if Tom would notice that she was wearing his present at last. He didn't, or if he did, he said nothing.

Laura began to chatter to fill the silence. She usually became quieter when she was anxious, but she found she could not bear the unasked questions between them. Perhaps it would be all right once they were in bed.

Yes, in bed — much less lumpy than the mattress she remembered from their honeymoon night — they moved close to each other. It was as if they were saying, as they settled into the familiar nooks of each other's bodies, "Oh, now I know who you are."

Expectantly, Laura waited for Tom's next move. When it didn't come, she raised her head slightly to look at him. His eyes were closed. She heard his deep even breathing, the profound sleep of the exhausted. Jet lag had won out over romance.

Their first night at the Copley, she had been the one to fall asleep while Tom was in the bathroom, elaborately showering and shaving for his bride. Now they were even. The balance sheet. In Winchester, when Mr. Richardson had given her money for stamps, it kept her from being able to balance the books. Not a good way to run a business, or to think of a loving relationship. Before Laura could think of a better way, she fell asleep.

The next morning, when she woke, Tom was already up and dressed, quietly turning the pages of the *Christian Science Monitor* in an armchair in the corner. The familiar puckers and wrinkles of their marriage fabric, concealed during their first reunion, reappeared as they discussed plans. Tom wanted to see the Museum of Science. He had never gotten around to visiting the science museum in Geneva, but the one in Boston was supposed to be even better. Laura wanted to visit the Isabella Stewart Gardner Museum. She hadn't been there since she had left Boston.

She still had a need to retrace the past, while Tom was already in the future. Once they would have compromised, gone to some place that neither of them wanted to go, or gone to both museums together as if they were Siamese twins.

Today Laura offered a solution that was breathtakingly simple. "Why don't you go to your museum and I'll go to mine?" She anticipated his next question. "And please don't ask me how I'm going to get there. I bought an MBTA map yesterday. The system's much simpler than in New York. All I have to do is take the outbound Green Line at Copley Square. The Arborway trolley comes above ground at Northeastern University, then goes out the Fenway to the Museum.

All *you* have to do is take the Green Line toward Lechmere. It lets you out directly in front of Science Park." How strange — and how gratifying — to be giving directions to Tom.

Tom was dubious. "Laura, are you sure you want to do it this way? We've been apart all summer. Don't you think we ought to spend the day together?"

"We are spending the day together. We just don't have to be together every minute. The Renaissance doesn't interest you. The future of nuclear energy bores me. Why should we pretend that we're interested when we're not?"

Her logic was unassailable, but Tom still looked uneasy. "The Green Line may be a trolley, but it's still underground for most of the way. Are you sure you can manage by yourself?" Perhaps Tom had needed to accompany her as much as she had needed to be accompanied.

"Before I married you I used to go to the Gardner Museum by myself all the time. How do you think I got there?" A question she could have asked of herself.

They arranged to meet at Quincy Market near Faneuil Hall for lunch. They parted at the entrance to the subway station, Tom still watching her doubtfully as if she might forget to cross at the green. How had he ever trusted her with their children?

In the Boston subways there were almost no graffiti, no threatening-looking passengers. None of the flamboyant self-exposing outfits of New Yorkers in the summer, either. People spoke neither to each other nor to themselves, and certainly not to strangers.

At Northeastern, just as she had predicted, the trolley emerged into the open, gliding smoothly past rows of sedate three-story buildings that had housed Bostonians for decades. The journey seemed tame after the excitement of the New York transportation system.

The Gardner Museum was, of course, exactly the same as

it had always been. In her will Mrs. Jack had commanded time to stop, and having a great deal of money, she had succeeded. The courtyard of the replica of a fifteenth-century Venetian palace was filled with flowers and sunlight, just as she had ordered. Laura sat for a long time at the edge of the courtyard, looking up at every arched window and balcony. Then she walked slowly from room to room, looking enviously at the set of gold Limoges, the harp, the tooled leather walls in the Veronese room. She peered at the Titians, Rembrandts, Botticellis, hidden in the dark corners. This too was part of the will — nothing to be moved from its accustomed place.

She could hear Tom's exasperated voice, "What's the point of putting real art in corners where you can't see it? Or of building an Italian palazzo four centuries late?" She turned down the volume of her husband's voice in her head, and returned to her bench in the courtyard. Mrs. Gardner doubtless had strolled among the flowers after dinner, sipping coffee from her Limoges demitasse.

Feeling more and more like a transportation expert, Laura switched trolleys at Prudential, got out at Government Center, and walked the short distance to Faneuil Hall, arriving just before Tom. He seemed astonished that she was actually there. Did he think that she would be lost forever beneath the streets of Boston?

They strolled through Quincy Market, which hadn't existed in its present form in their Boston days. Booths on either side filled with every conceivable kind of food that could be eaten while walking. They bought a large plastic container filled with cubes of fresh watermelon, berries, and pineapple, and carried it before them like a talisman to ward off the tempting aromas, while they made up their minds.

Laura was acutely aware of how she and Tom made even the simplest decision (if indeed there was such a thing). Whether to eat while walking or to look for a table while eating the sloppier foods — her preference. Whether to buy the same dessert, or try two different kinds and sample each other's — Tom's preference.

I don't remember that we used to disagree this much, Laura thought. Or is it that we just kept quiet about it, the one feeling weaker at the moment giving in, the other triumphing?

After lunch Laura wanted to ride the Red Line to Harvard Square and look at the glass flowers in the Peabody Museum. Tom wanted to look at Boston from the top of the John Hancock Tower. Tom looked so anxious, as if he were afraid she might be going to suggest they spend their afternoon separately, that she agreed to forgo the glass flowers. They walked to Park Street. Laura led the way, enjoying the continuous look of surprise on Tom's face.

Then, clutching the roses Tom had bought her from a flower vendor in front of the Old South Church ("Aren't real flowers nicer than glass ones?" he asked), Laura ascended to the top of the tower and saw Boston spread out below like a child's drawing of a city.

The sunlight glinted on tiny sailboats on the Charles. Cars on the streets far below looked like the cars in Jeff's Matchbox collection. Behind them a voice told them what they were looking at, and what they would have been looking at if there had been such a tower two hundred years ago.

"They're always lecturing," Tom said with sudden irritation. "Can't they leave us alone and let us look at things in our own way? Does it matter so much if we don't know what we're seeing?"

"No, it doesn't," Laura said. "Let's get out of here."

Acting in concert at last, as if they had one mind, one body, they left their electronic instructor, descended to the ground floor, returned to their bedroom across the square, and began to take off their clothes.

Laura lay naked except for the tiny edelweiss on the chain around her neck.

"It looks very sexy there," Tom said softly, "nestled between the Alps."

"More like foothills," said Laura, but Tom was too busy kissing her breasts to answer. She touched his chest with her fingers and her lips until his nipples too stood erect.

Desire stirred between them, as it had not for many months. They didn't have to ask each other (as Masters and Johnson had suggested that the couples of America should) what they liked and what they didn't like. In twelve years of lovemaking, they had learned. They knew how to indicate, by small thrusts of the body, placings of the hands, what they would like more of, what less, where and when. Laura found herself less passive, more aware of her partner and what he might be needing, and for this she silently thanked Enid. If Tom noticed the change in her lovemaking, he said nothing.

They lay back, finally, on the double bed and grinned at each other. Tom rubbed his lips lightly across her navel, their sign that sex was, for the moment, over.

"This is one thing we do together very well," he said smugly. And she, comfortable and content, had to agree.

∾ 24 ∾

In the middle of the night Laura woke Tom. Automatically his hand began to caress her buttocks. Half asleep, he was ready to begin again. Gently she pushed his hand aside. "Tom, wake up. We need to talk."

He sat up, looking around the room in bewilderment. "Why? What's happening? What's wrong?"

"Nothing. Everything. I don't know. That's why we have to talk."

Now he was awake. Looking at her, he saw that this was serious. The day of reckoning. He had known it was coming, but he had hoped it could be postponed. It would be better to be alert. He splashed water on his face, put on his robe, and placed himself in the room's one comfortable chair.

Laura was disconcerted. She had thought they would have their discussion in the warm rumpled bed, lying next to each other. Tom was looking at her as if she were part of a college debating team, and he was assigned to take notes for the rebuttal. She murmured, "Not like that. We're not adversaries. Can't you come back to bed? You seem so far away over there."

"Why don't you come over here? Then we'll both be comfortable."

There was an invisible line in the middle of the room that neither was willing to cross. It had not been there when they had gotten into bed together — what they each had wanted then had been identical.

Tom was waiting. She was the one who had said she wanted to talk. She knew that if it were up to him, they would never have a discussion. They would just take up where they had left off. But that would not do. A few things, at least, had to be said. And now that the sex part was all right, perhaps it was safe to talk.

Tentatively she began. "Do you remember the old days, when we used to tell each other everything?"

Tom smiled. "Yes. I've been remembering them all the time I was in Geneva. And today on Beacon Hill." He sighed, a sound Laura had rarely heard from him. "If only we could go back."

That's what she had been wishing a little while ago, when she had come to Boston, when she had asked him to come. Now for the hard part. She braced herself. "I'm not sure I want to."

She felt him stiffen. "What do you mean?" His voice was calm, but his hand shook slightly. "That you want to live by yourself?"

"No. But I could." Even to herself she sounded cocky, like Peter Pan showing off before the Darling children, when they were still firmly anchored to the floor.

"I know you could." His voice was carefully neutral. How could she talk to such a well-bred mask? She had thrown off hers, but he was still hiding.

Laura ventured across the invisible line and sat beside Tom on the arm of the chair. To her immense surprise, she saw that there were tears in his eyes. Why had she assumed that only she was grieving for their past?

"Tom," she said softly, "we can't go back. It was beautiful then — maybe not as beautiful as we remember — but still very good. Too much has happened. We're not the same people."

He nodded, knowing this was true. Laura had changed more than he. She was now someone who could take care of herself if she had to — and even if she didn't. Someone who might not need other people.

"What about me?" he said, not meaning to. "What about us?"

"That's what I want to talk about." Laura had a sudden inspiration. "It's what editors are always saying about manuscripts. Our marriage has possibilities, but it needs work."

"You mean it's basically sound, but it needs revision?"

She nodded, glad that he seemed interested in emendation.

He was definitely interested, and once more in control. "The first step is to list what's wrong with the marriage now." He sounded as if he were drawing up a research proposal.

"What do you mean?"

"Just what I said. We have to tell each other whatever has been bothering us. Get it all out into the open."

She wasn't sure she liked the sound of that. It didn't sound like one of Tom's suggestions. Had the company been running group sensitivity sessions in Geneva? She moved from the arm of the chair back to the bed.

They had never had a discussion like this before. Once they began, who knew where this hazardous game might take them?

"All right, Laura, why don't you begin?"

"No, you. It was your idea."

She could barely see him sitting across the room from her in the dark, wearing the brown Viyella robe she had bought for his birthday three years ago. She felt as if they were putting each other on trial. The case of Thomas Stone versus Laura Stone. But who would be the jury? And what had been the crime?

He cleared his throat. "Ever since we first met, I've felt that you looked down on me. You were the cultured one, the one with taste. I was the clod." There was a moment of silence. "Your turn."

Laura's voice trembled slightly. "To look down on people, you have to be aware of them. You haven't been aware of me as a separate person for a long time. You think of me only as your wife, or as your children's mother."

"That's not true. But you've been totally absorbed in the children. They've used up all your time and energy. You've chosen them over me."

Their voices were beginning to rise. It was Laura's turn. "You've chosen your work over me. You care more about what's happening in a test tube than what's happening in your family."

"You don't respect my research. You never ask how it's going, what I'm working on." Tom continued, no longer taking turns, as if once begun he couldn't be held back by their middle-of-the-night rules. "I left Geneva four days early in order to be with you. I probably gave up my chance to teach at the university next summer."

"That's not fair. I didn't ask you to leave."

It was as if he hadn't heard her. "I made you fresh coffee and brought it to you in bed. But you were sleeping somewhere else."

"You know perfectly well where I was sleeping," she almost shouted. "And what's so great about making a cup of coffee? I've made coffee for you every morning for the past twelve years."

The flood of their grievances was carrying them past summer seminars and cups of coffee. Tom spoke quietly, almost menacingly.

"What's so great about forgetting you have a husband? You're so involved in finding yourself, in making new friends, that you've forgotten about me. About our marriage."

She heard her own voice making the accusation she had

promised herself never to make. "I'm not the only one who's made new friends."

Now they were skating on thin ice indeed. They both retreated, appalled at what had almost been said. If they continued in this way, there would be nothing left of the marriage to emend.

Tom crossed over and sat on the bed next to her. "Laura," he said, stroking her hair, almost as if he were unaware that he was touching her, "I never meant to hurt you."

She said nothing, but she did not move away.

"I've been disappointed in myself, in my life. Scared that maybe this is all there's going to be."

Laura sighed. "I was going to say almost the same to you."

They were both quiet now, thinking of all they had hoped to be, separately and together. Laura was aware of the ticking of Tom's traveling clock on the bedside table, of someone letting the water out of a bathtub, the murmur of the television next door.

They were novices at the art of fighting. By the standards of marital warfare, this was only a skirmish, but for them, so unused to putting anger into words, it was a major confrontation. There were many important questions they had not discussed tonight, or had only skirted. But at least they had begun.

Were the hurtful accusations they had made about each other true? It was almost impossible to tell. At least that was how each of them was feeling. And not saying. They had been in two different marriages without knowing it, each feeling neglected, uncherished by the other.

Tom took off his robe and put his arm around Laura. "We're not so bad."

She nodded. "We're much better than some." It would be so easy to lean against his shoulder and stop talking, but she had one more point to make. "Tom, when we get back to New York, it's got to be different."

"I know. And it will be."

She couldn't tell from his tone whether he welcomed or feared the changes that were coming. She was touched that he was willing to try. "And when we need to, not all the time, but when we need to, we'll talk to each other about how we're feeling."

This kind of conversation was difficult for Tom, much harder than it was for her. Now a paralyzing wave of sleepiness swept over him. "But next time, Laura, could we start the discussion a little earlier?"

She was not feeling sleepy at all. She hadn't felt so full of energy and bounce in a long time. But Tom was right. It was the middle of the night, time to go back to bed. They climbed back under the covers, their bodies fitting together like pieces of a jigsaw puzzle. This time they made love leisurely, lingeringly, like loving friends who expected to be together for a long time.

Just before they drifted off, she said, "Remember the first night we were here."

Tom's voice was very faint. He was almost asleep. "We didn't know each other at all then."

Or now either, she thought. But they were learning.

∞ 25 ∞

THE ATTEMPT TO RECREATE THE PAST is over. Ordinary life begins the next morning when the phone rings at eight o'clock. Tom reaches out and picks it up, answering in a sleep-fogged voice. Laura tries to stay submerged in a particularly delightful dream.

It is Jeff calling from camp. Laura is instantly alert, sitting up, reaching out her hand for the phone. Tom waves her away, indicating that he will take care of it. She is left to piece the situation together from his side of the conversation.

Jeff is suffering. His best friend has just told him that he no longer wants to be his best friend. He has chosen someone else, an older boy from the next bunk. Laura can hear his voice as he tells Tom the story, trying with only partial success to keep back his sobs.

Again she reaches for the phone. Her son is in distress. He needs her.

But Tom seems to be managing very well. He does not try to minimize Jeff's pain, to tell him that he should forget about it. Instead he listens. He tells Jeff that he knows how he feels. Nobody likes to be rejected. He will probably feel unhappy for quite a while. Then he may find a new friend. Or his old one may change his mind.

Jeff's voice is calmer now. He is speaking in regular sentences, not frantic, choking phrases. Tom hands the phone to Laura. "He wants to talk to you."

"Hi, Mom." Jeff sounds exactly as he always does on the phone. "How are you?"

Amazed, pleased. She didn't know that Tom could be like this with his children. Chagrined. She has never given him the chance to be.

Seated on the plane next to Tom, her thigh placed companionably against his, Laura reads the headline in the newspaper that the flight attendant has just handed her. SNIPER STRAFES DOWNTOWN BUS. She reads on. The passengers and the driver huddle terrified on the floor. Miraculously, no one is injured.

She thinks, Boston is not safe, buses are not safe. Even marriage is not safe. Almost as dangerous as gunfire, the slow erosion of a marriage left unattended. Like the passengers on the bus, she and Tom are survivors. How much more than that waits to be seen, but she is hopeful.

Looking up from his journal of research chemistry, Tom glances at the headlines. Violence everywhere. No place safe, not even bed. Will I ever ask Laura exactly what happened this summer, and with whom? Probably not. Wiser to leave well enough alone. Not like it used to be, but much better than it was. And it may get even better. How to explain at the office why I changed my reservations at the last minute? No need to explain. None of their damn business. Just mine and Laura's.

He leans over the arm of Laura's seat. "Do you think Jeff will recover?"

She nods. "It was probably the shock. Being chosen Camper

of the Year made him think that everybody had to love him."

Tom smiles. "He wrote me about that. He seemed very excited."

"What about Kathy? Do you think she'll be proud of her brother or jealous?"

"Both. We'll have to pay a little more attention to her when they come home."

They smile at each other, go back to their reading.

Laura, thinking. Being parents of children is not enough, but it is still a lot. Alan would have whirled apart into anxious fragments long ago if he didn't have to keep himself together for Sandy. And Enid — she had said Sarah and her work were her center.

Quick slides of Enid in the museum giving orders. In the pool. In bed, naked, laughing. Holding Laura's hand. Telling her she can do whatever she wants to do. Enid will be home in a few weeks. And Alan is probably calling right now, wanting to read his revised manuscript to her over the telephone. Her new friends of the summer, of the fall.

Laura, writing in the journal she has decided to keep in this new phase of her life, "We give each other space. We don't hassle each other, breathe down each other's necks, peer into each other's psyches like the desperate uncouples do. Too much intensity for me in the single life. I need the privacy of a long-term marriage, where we live and let live. Important to live, though. Take some chances, try some new ways. Even with one's husband."

Tom looks at Laura. He wonders what she is writing, but he doesn't ask. A good person. A person to hold on to. He thinks he really loves her.

She thinks the same about him. And begins to make a list of things to do before the children come home.